World Wide Web: how to design and construct Web pages

Second edition

Routledge
Taylor & Francis Group

LONDON AND NEW YORK

First Published 2000 by Aslib, The Association for Information Management

Published 2017 by Routledge
2 Park Square, Milton Park, Abingdon,
Oxon OX14 4RN
711 Third Avenue, New York, NY 10017, USA

Routledge is an imprint of the Taylor & Francis Group, an informa business

ISBN 13:978-0-85142-435-4 (pbk)

World Wide Web: how to design and construct Web pages

Second edition

Phil Bradley

Is your organisation a corporate member of Aslib?

Aslib, The Association for Information Management, is a world class corporate membership organisation with over 2000 members in some 70 countries. Aslib actively promotes best practice in the management of information resources. It lobbies on all aspects of the management of, and legislation concerning, information at local, national and international levels.

Aslib provides consultancy and information services, professional development training, conferences, specialist recruitment, Internet products, and publishes primary and secondary journals, conference proceedings, directories and monographs.

Series Editor

Sylvia Webb is a well-known consultant, author and lecturer in the information management field. Her first book, *Creating an Information Service*, now in its third edition, was published by Aslib and has sold in over forty countries. She has experience of working in both the public and private sectors, ranging from public libraries to national and international organisations. She has also been a lecturer at Ashridge Management College, specialising in management and interpersonal skills, which led to her second book, *Personal Development in Information Work*, also published by Aslib. She has served on a number of government advisory bodies and is past Chair of the former Information and Library Services Lead Body, now the Information Services National Training Organisation which develops National and Scottish Vocational Qualifications (NVQs and SVQs) for the LIS profession. She is actively involved in professional education and training and is also a former Vice-President of the Institute of Information Scientists. As well as being editor of this series, Sylvia Webb has written three of the Know How Guides: *Making a charge for library and information services*, *Preparing a guide to your library and information service* and *Knowledge management: linchpin of change*.

A complete listing of all titles in the series can be found at the back of this volume.

About the author

Phil Bradley is an information professional who has worked in the field of electronic publications for the last 20 years. Phil is currently an Internet Consultant, and he runs a variety of training courses in the field of the Internet and writing web pages in particular. He also acts as the Web author for a number of different clients, designing, creating and maintaining their web sites for them.

As well as running training courses and maintaining web pages Phil is a regular speaker at information related conferences, both in the UK and abroad, and he also writes on the subject of the Internet for a number of different publishers and in professional journals.

Finally, when not using the Internet for work related purposes, he uses it to explore his own interests of the American Civil War, science fiction and Everton Football Club.

His website address is http://www.philb.com if you want to obtain more information, or to contact him.

Contents

Introduction

This guide is designed to give you a basic background to both the World Wide Web (also known as the Web or WWW), and how to design and create your own pages which can be published for the world to see.

The first few sections of the book will provide you with the theory behind the creation of the Web, why it is so popular, and the type of information that you can locate on it. The rest of the book will guide you through the creation of a simple home page, with graphics, links and so on, in order to make it attractive to viewers.

The final chapter will list some of the resources that are available to you which will help you in the creation of more complicated pages.

No prior knowledge of the Web is assumed, and the reader is expected to have no more than a passing familiarity with the Internet in general. However, if have already spent some time using the Internet and the Web in particular, you may wish to simply skim-read Chapters 1 - 2 and move straight onto the design and writing sections of the book.

Writing Web pages does not require any kind of programming background, and while you can make use of specialist tools to write pages, the guidelines you will find in this book will ensure that you will be able to write them using no more than a standard word processor, although to view them on the screen you will need to make use of a browser such as Netscape or Microsoft Internet Explorer. This guide does not attempt to cover every single aspect of writing Web pages (it would need to be twenty times as large!), but it does cover many points that you will need to know and understand in order to create good pages. It will also cover all of the major mark-up tags you will need to know in order to create a functional page.

This is the second edition of this particular title, and I have updated it to include new mark-up tags, new resources and so on.

Other titles in the Know How series which complement this one are:

Intranets and push technology: creating an information-sharing environment by Paul Pedley, Aslib, 1999

How to promote your web site effectively by Mark Kerr, Aslib, 1999

The Internet for library and information service professionals, 3rd ed., by Andy Dawson, Aslib, forthcoming 2000

Acknowledgements

The first edition of this title was written by myself and my colleague Anna Smith, who was unable to collaborate with me on the second edition due to other work commitments. However, I have re-used some of her text in this edition so would like to pay my thanks to her. Thanks are also due to my many friends and colleagues, and also visitors to my pages who make valuable suggestions and contributions, and also to my clients who let me loose on their sites!

Finally, thanks are as always due to my wife, who valiantly puts up with my Internet addiction. Jill – this is for you, with my love.

1. What is the Internet, and where does the Web fit into it?

Although for many of us the Internet has appeared on the scene in the last few years, it has been around for a lot longer than that; the origins can be traced back to the late 1960s. The American military wanted to have some way of being able to talk to itself in the event of World War 3, and an effective communication system was designed by American academics, who were also quick to see the value of such a system for themselves.

As a result, over the next few years more and more academic sites gained access to this new network, and shared emails back and forth and were also able to make files available for download to different sites, provide access to library catalogues and so on.

As time went on, more and more academic institutions around the world became involved with this fledgling network, and it became a truly international system. No-one is quite sure as to the origin of the word 'Internet', but I rather like the idea that it was coined because the system became an INTERnational NETwork of networks. By the late 1980's the Internet had grown far beyond what had originally been envisaged, but it was still essentially the province of academics and computer buffs. One of the main reasons for this is that although there were a lot of utilities available to use and search the Internet, pass email back and forth and so on, these utilities were usually DOS or UNIX based and were command line driven. This was before the days of graphical interfaces which simplified the whole process, so the utilities were complicated and very user-unfriendly; similar in fact to the early interfaces that information professionals used when searching online databases.

By the late 1980's the lack of a friendly interface was becoming more and more of a problem and Tim Berners-Lee, of the European Laboratory for Particle Physics, also known as CERN (the Centre Européenne pour la Recherche Nucléaire), developed the first Web servers and clients. Initially, he wanted a better way of allowing the high energy physics community to communicate easily and quickly. He coined the term 'Web' in 1990 to describe his vision of a giant spider's web which spanned the globe, with each thread of information and knowledge linked to each other. In order to achieve this vision, he made use of the concept of 'hypertext', a term coined by Theodore Nelson in 1965 to define his idea of all knowledge being available in a single database, or browsable format.

What is hypertext?

Essentially, hypertext is the ultimate concept in browsing or serendipity. Imagine for a moment a standard encyclopaedia, with all its entries and photographs in the usual linear format. You choose articles to read via the index, and if you are half way through reading a particular article you may well see references to other articles or footnotes which point you in other directions. Now, in a paper format it is necessary for you to locate the new article and turn to it, perhaps leaving a bookmark at the first entry to allow you to go back to it later after you have finished reading the new article. You may well then locate a third or fourth article, depending on your subject of study, and the depth to which you want to research it. Before very long you have read or skimmed a number of articles, leaving a lot of bookmarks behind you, in order to fully explore the subject that you are interested in. You have stopped reading the encyclopaedia in a linear fashion and instead are exploring a concept or subject following your own train of thought, rather than that placed upon you by the compilers of the reference work.

You can of course expand this concept from one single reference book to your entire information centre or library. If you are asked to obtain information on a subject you do not start at the first book on the shelf and work your way through to the last one, or until you find the information you need. Instead, you start your exploration in one source which in turn leads you to another and yet another, and you may well have ended up having interrogated several books, journals, newspapers, videos or photographs until you have answered your query to your satisfaction and that of your client.

Therefore, the concept behind hypertext is not new, and is one that you will have already been using all of your professional life, and before. However, implementing this across a world wide network was a new concept, and herein lies the strength of the Web. The use of hypertext in documents with links from one to another, or from text to graphic or moving images is the ultimate in browsing or serendipity. It is also extraordinarily easy to use; if this were a hypertext document on the Web I could quite easily have created links from particular terms to a glossary for example. To find further references to, or information about hypertext, I could under line the word 'hypertext' and you could click on it with your mouse and be immediately taken directly to the glossary. Then you could read what you wanted to about the subject there and either come back to exactly this point in the book to carry on reading, or click on another term and be taken elsewhere within the whole document. Of course, if this was a Web page instead of a book, I could also have put a link into other books or pages that covered the same subject, or even to a moving image of me talking to you about the subject!

What does the Web cover?

For those who are unfamiliar, or only have a passing knowledge of the Web, this section briefly discusses the kind of information that you will commonly find available. It will also help you decide if the material that you have is suitable for publishing on the Web, or if your organisation can profit in some way from doing this.

You can find anything and everything on the Web, in one form or another. Professional organisations, commercial companies and individuals have all made data available across the Web for people to make use of, or simply to wonder why anyone would put it up in the first place!

At one end of the spectrum, you will find data from the Library of Congress or the British Library, both of which are making data available to information professionals and the layperson alike. Then there are organisations in particular fields which are promoting themselves across the Internet; often, but not always, with an eye to making money. Then there are home pages produced by individuals who simply want to claim a little section of the web for themselves.

All this information is made available in a glorious, uncontrolled mish-mash of the subtle, garish and downright unreadable. You will find some Web pages that are utilitarian in the extreme, and tell you little more than the name, address and interests of the organisation that put them up. At the other end of the spectrum you will find pages that are little less than works of art in their own right, with pages that provide you with information (high quality or not) in between. All of this occurs because quite simply, no-one owns the Internet, and so each individual or organisation can place almost whatever they want to on the Web. I say 'almost' because laws do exist that cover the Internet, despite what you might have heard to the contrary. For example, I'd be breaking the law if I published libellous material in hard copy, and I'd also be doing so if I put the same information onto a web page. However, other than obvious exceptions such as that, anyone is free to publish whatever information they want to.

You may have heard that advertising is frowned upon, but this is only really true in the area of USENET newsgroups, which form a distinctive and separate part of the Internet, unconnected with Web pages (although of course they can be accessed via them). The Web however positively thrives on commerce; traditional and electronic publishers have made their data available across the Web, which can be searched and items purchased electronically; I do most of my shopping via Internet supermarkets, and my credit card can certainly attest that most of my book purchases are made this way as well!

Consequently, if you want to take commercial advantage of the Web you are free to do so, and you can sell anything you deem appropriate; your home page can be your shop window on the Internet, or your virtual catalogue. It is however entirely up to you as to how you achieve this, and you must make sure that your pages are of sufficient interest for people to visit them, and more importantly, return to them time and time again.

On the other hand, you may simply wish to make information available to your potential users, and many organisations do just that. Given that millions of people access the Web every single day you can be assured that whatever information you make available, it will be found useful by any number of people.

The explosion of publishing on the Web is quite remarkable; it has become one of the most important means of publishing in today's world. Any figures I can provide will be almost meaningless by the time you read this, but just to give you a flavour there are currently (July 2000) over 1 billion web pages available, with another million being published every single day. I fully expect that when you're reading this book there will be over a billion pages that can be accessed from your computer.

In summary therefore, whatever you do, whatever the organisation that you work for, you can make use of the Web to provide information, make sales or simply to provide you with publicity. The extent to which you are successful at doing this will depend very much on the creation of your web pages; you can have very useful information, or a superb project, but if it's badly presented, or the page takes too long to load, your potential readers or customers will look elsewhere for the information they are after.

The rest of this book will look in-depth at how you can best produce your web pages to ensure that visitors come to visit you, rather than going to the competition (however you define that).

2. Using the World Wide Web as a Web author

I will make the assumption that you have a computer that is already connected to the Internet, you have a web browser (and it will probably be either be a Netscape or Microsoft product), and that you have already spent some time using the Web for work, pleasure, or both. In the first edition of this book I spent some considerable time explaining how to use your browser, but I think it's now safe to say that you already know how to do this, so why have I still included a section on it?

Until now, you have been using the Web as a user, looking for information, rather than as a Web author in your own right. You have been a consumer, rather than a producer, and in order to be able to produce information successfully you need to work out what your particular audience wants, and the best place to start that research is with yourself.

Try a little experiment; if possible, stop reading this book now and go away and spend 10 or 15 minutes using the Web, perhaps using a search engine to find something useful, visit a few sites and follow one or two links. While I hope you find useful information, that's not really the point of this exercise. Try and keep a little part of your mind objective, acting as an observer to watch exactly what it is that you're doing. If you don't have a computer available, or you're reading this on the train for example, just spend a few minutes thinking back to the last time that you used the Web. When you've done that, come back and continue reading.

Right, I hope that you enjoyed that. Let's now take a look at the things you might have done or thought about while you were doing this, and how you can make use of what you did as an aid to designing your own web pages.

1. You opened your browser

Which browser was it? As I said above, it was probably produced by either Netscape or Microsoft, although it is quite possible that it was neither of these – there are at least a dozen different browsers available for people to use. Which version of the browser were you using? Hopefully, it was a recent version, either 4.x or 5.x, but it is quite possible that it was an older version; I still see and hear of people using a version 2.x of whichever browser they have, or they're using the version that came with their computer and they haven't upgraded.

The importance of the browser cannot be over estimated; it is your window onto a web page and the way in which it interprets the commands that have been given to it from the web page will affect the way in which you see that particular page. You might have noticed that some of the pages that you looked at said that they were enhanced to work with a particular browser, or even a version of that browser. Did you notice anything odd about the page? This might have been because you were using a browser that the author hadn't taken into account when designing their pages, giving you a less than wonderful viewing experience. As a Web author, one of the first things that you have to realise is that you cannot completely control how someone views your pages; they may have an older browser that doesn't understand some of the commands that you've placed into your page, or they might have decided to turn off the automatic loading of graphics for example.

As a Web author you will need to ensure that your pages work well with as many different browsers as possible, and with as many different versions of those browsers. Consequently, if you commonly use Netscape, acquire a copy of Explorer or vice versa, and spend some time looking at Web pages using that. If you already use both, get hold of yet another browser and view pages using that for a while. After a while it will become second nature to consider looking at your web pages through the eyes of an audience, who are using different browsers, rather than assuming that everyone will see your pages in exactly the way that you wrote them.

2. You may have gone to your bookmark/favourites utility to call up a site

If you did this, was it clear to you exactly where you were going to visit, just from the information available in that utility? You may have some entries which are quite clear on this point, but it's equally possible you'll find some entries that are vague or unclear, forcing you to go back and visit the site to find out why you bookmarked it in the first place! We'll discuss a little later how you can ensure that the bookmark or favourite utilities can work in your favour, rather than against you.

3. You might have typed in a URL (Uniform Resource Locator) and hit enter to go directly to an often visited site

How do you remember the URL? I imagine, if you're anything like me, it's because it's a short one, or memorable, or both. I'm willing to bet that it's not a very long or obscure one. This is something else that we'll look at in some detail.

4. Perhaps you went to your favourite search engine and did a search

What sort of search did you do? Was it simply a series of words, or perhaps a phrase? Alternatively, it might have been much more complicated. Whatever it was that you did, were you happy with the results that you got? Did you get any really good hits, or did you get some that just didn't seem appropriate at all? When writing web pages you'll need to consider how people are going to find your site, and to do your level best to ensure that your web pages come up as close to the top of the list of returned sites. If they don't, you're going to be missing a perfect opportunity to attract people to your site. Furthermore, did you consider that there are a lot of sites out there which are not indexed by search engines? It's been estimated that about 400,000,000 web pages have not been registered with search engines, so they are in many cases completely invisible; they might as well not exist. Registering with search engines is not a difficult thing to do, and I'll show you how to do it, but once again it's crucial that you do.

5. You visited the site of your choice

How long did it take for the web page to load? If the page loaded quickly (and by quickly I mean in less than 15 seconds) I expect you were happy to wait for those few seconds. If it took much longer than that, I imagine you might have begun to get a little restless, and much longer again I'd say that you probably didn't wait for the page to load (unless you were really desperate to see it), and you visited another site instead. When writing web pages you have to ensure that something appears on the viewer's screen as soon as possible, or you'll run the risk that they too, will not twiddle their thumbs, but will go somewhere else instead.

6. You looked at the site (obviously!)

What did you like about it? Perhaps it was clearly laid out, easy to follow, nice or attractive use of graphics and so on. On the other hand, you might not have enjoyed your viewing experience; graphics may not have loaded, you might have had to visit several links to get to the information that you wanted, or the information might have been out of date (and did you know that?)

The visual appearance of a Web site is one of the most difficult things of all to quantify; what is a delightful experience for one person is a nightmare for another. Your idea of what constitutes a 'good' web site is going to be different from that of your friends or colleagues. As an author, you'll have to make all of those choices for yourself, and get feedback from other people before adjusting your pages accordingly. Remember that you can't please all of the people all of the time, but there are certain things you can keep in the back of your mind to ensure that most of the people are pleased most of the time, and we'll discuss these later as well.

7. Did you trust the information that you found?

Not an obvious point this, by any manner or means. Many people will simply accept that, if they see something on a Web page, it must be true. If you're an information professional you will of course be wary of taking information for granted; it might be out of date or just plain wrong. So, how did you decide that the information you found was of good quality, or alternatively, that it might be suspect? What hints or clues were you able to take from the page or site to provide you with assurances that the data could be trusted? You'll need to make sure that you provide your users with that sort of information, and don't fall into the trap of assuming that they will trust the data they find, because many of them won't do that.

8. Did you follow any links?

What attracted you to follow a particular link? How was the link made available – was it a link within the text, and <u>simply underlined like this</u>? Did you find that more 'reader friendly' than a link that said <u>click here</u>? It's a small, but important point; as well as providing links they should be made available within the context of the page, or they may well stick out like the proverbial sore thumb. Or perhaps it was a graphic – was it clear there was a link, or did you find it by a happy accident? Links are a very important element of any Web page, both internally to the entire site and also externally to other sites. You will need to consider the pages that you produce and decide what links you want, where they go to, how to provide them, and what you need to do to link to sites that having nothing directly to do with you.

9. Was any multimedia used?

By this I mean, were there any film clips, sound files, or even animated images on the page? Did you like them, find them useful or were they just an irritant? If you were really unlucky, you might have stumbled across a page that automatically started playing music to you. If it didn't send you insane within a few moments you have more patience than I do! Furthermore, were there some multimedia files that you couldn't load, because you didn't have the appropriate utility, and if that was the case, how did you feel about that?

I could carry on, but I hope that I've managed to make my point. All too often we just act as consumers of data, and if you never intend to write a web page there's nothing wrong with that of course. However, since you're intending to publish information for yourself (and you wouldn't be reading this book unless you were), one of the first things that you need to do is to start to think like an author. The best way of doing that is to become much more objective about the pages that you look at. Squirrel away information about the pages you visit, or make a note of what things work for you and those which just make you want to leave the page immediately. All of this information will be useful to you in the future. I can guarantee that you'll never look at web pages in quite the same way again!

3. First steps in designing your Web page

At this point it might be useful if I clarify a few terms for you, since I'll be using them extensively from now on. (Of course, if this was a hyperlinked text you could click on particular words and I wouldn't need to do this!).

I've already used several, so let's use those as our starting point. I've mentioned 'pages' quite a lot. By a 'page' I mean an amount of data that your browser displays on the screen for you to look at. This might be a very short page, only a few lines in length, or alternatively the page could be several, or indeed many screens full of text, graphics and other information. The title of this chapter is 'First steps in designing your Web site'. Your web site is your collection of Web pages, held together by the links that you have between them. Even if you only have one or two pages, together they go to make up your site. At the other extreme some Web sites will have literally thousands of web pages linked together, but it's still just a Web site. I also use the term 'home page' as well. This is a slightly different page, because it should (hopefully!) be your introductory page, which tells people about the site, the type of information they can expect to find in it, and various navigation aids to move around the site. However, you also need to remember that it

might not be the first page on your site that someone visits; a search engine might return a different
page, or someone else might have linked to another
of your pages, and you have little or no control over
this. Nonetheless, I'll still use the phrase 'home page'
to make the distinction between that and other
pages, because the home page should be doing a
significantly different job to the rest of the site. I've
also used words such as 'codes' or 'instructions'.
This is a clumsy way of talking about HTML tags,
and HTML stands for HyperText Markup Language. HTML tags are used by the web author to
instruct the browser to correctly display information on the screen, such as centring text, or em-
boldening text for example. Now, having got that
out of the way, let's start looking at how you design
your site.

3.1 Initial Design

For the time being, let's forget some of the technical
aspects of creating pages and concentrate on some
information background; what do you want your
site to do, who do you expect to visit it, and how
will all the different pages link together to create
the whole site? You might want to sit down with
paper and pen, or brainstorm with a few colleagues
to come up with some ideas. Now, I know that you
want to get right ahead and start creating pages,
but I can assure you that the more time you can
devote to the design stage, the easier it will be to
write your pages and create your site. If you rush
in and start writing pages immediately it won't take

very long before the site becomes messy and you'll get confused – I know; it's happened to me!

3.1.1 Purpose of the site

What do you want your site to do? Is it primarily an information tool to alert people to you, or your organisation and what it does? Or do you want to use it to advertise products, allow people to contact you directly to order items? Perhaps you want to provide access to many other pages that cover your subject area. Alternatively, you might just want to publish information about yourself and your interests; the "15 minutes of fame" syndrome (and there's nothing wrong with that at all!) Whichever of these applies, or indeed a combination of them, you'll need to make a list of the things that you want people to know. At this stage, just scribble them down on a sheet or two of paper, and we'll talk about arranging them later.

3.1.2 An organisational site

Start by asking yourself what sort of information **you** look for on an organisational site; this should immediately give you a good list. However, I'll also give you a list of some of the things that I think are important, and surprisingly, although there are several obvious points here, many organisations forget them when putting their sites together, so I make no apology for including them.

Logo

If you've got a logo, make sure that you use it! It can be one of the most effective ways of immediately giving a level of authority to your site; if people recognise the logo they will start to feel at home on the site, and you'll have overcome any initial resistance that they might otherwise have. You may decide to use the same logo that you use on hard copy materials that you produce or alternatively you could go for a slightly different version, because of course you're dealing with a different medium. Don't make the logo too different though, or you'll defeat the purpose of the exercise!

Contact details

Many people visit a Web site because they want to get a phone number to ring you up and talk to you; I know that I do, and I'm sure you're no different. However, it is surprising that so many organisations omit this valuable information; the only reason that I can think of is that they get so fixated on the Web as an electronic medium they forget that people might want to physically visit them, or fax information through to them. As well as the basics of address, phone and fax numbers you might want to include appropriate email addresses, a map showing your location, or indeed a photograph of your building, if you think it will help people find you.

Function of the organisation

What do you actually **do**? Does your organisation have a mission statement for example? If possible, identify some key words that clearly indicate who you are, what you do, and what subject areas you cover. While you're doing this, try and create a short sentence of no more than 25 words that also says who you are, and what you do. We'll come back to this later, since it will be one of the important ways that people are able to find you.

Graphical images

Graphics are talked about later, but for now, simply consider what would be useful for people to see. If you're producing a site about your university, it might be nice to include pictures of what the campus looks like. Alternatively, you might want some images of products that you produce, or a picture of when the Queen visited for example. Make sure the pictures you choose actually inform/entertain visitors; there is nothing worse than waiting ages for a graphic to load which doesn't add anything to the site.

Content

This is of course the biggest area, and the one that you'll have to spend longest working with. Gather together examples of all of the literature that your organisation produces, and start to think about which of them would be useful additions to your site. The old joke about selling a property (location, location and location) can easily be adapted for the Web, only in this instance it's content, content and content. As we'll see later on (Chapter 4), it is perhaps not a good idea to simply decide to transfer this content to your Web site; you will probably have to make several alterations to the data to make it suitable for the web, but at this stage just use the material to give you ideas of what you should include.

Links to other sites

You might want to guide your audience to other web sites by adding links to those sites from your own pages. This can be a powerful weapon in getting return visits; if people know that you are producing useful information, so that they don't have to, they are more likely to return to you in order to reap the benefits of your hard work.

These are just a few of the things that you'll want to consider at this early stage. If you run out of ideas, you might want to go back and visit a few sites and look at what similar organisations have done with their own materials, and jot down a few further ideas. What you then do with that information is covered later in Chapter 4.

3.1.3 An advertising site

As well as all the information mentioned above you will also want to consider the best ways of presenting your products. How you do this will depend entirely on the product, of course. If you produce reports or similar publications it might be an idea to provide a sample chapter, or table of contents. On the other hand, if you sell software, you might want people to be able to download a version of software, or access to a technical support bulletin board. If you produce candlesticks, have images on your site so that people can see what they look like. The list is really endless, and the best advice I can give is, once again, think about what you would expect to see, and look at competitors' sites to see how they've solved the problem (or not, as may be the case, which will give you even more useful information!).

3.1.4 A personal home page

Nothing wrong with doing one of these of course, and it might be a good place to start experimenting. What you decide to talk about is entirely up to you, but remember that it has got to be interesting! Consequently, it might be a good idea to produce information about your hobbies, favourite film star or author and so on. To give a personal example, my mother has built a doll's house, and her site has photographs of it, information on how she created it and so on. She gets lots of visitors and has had some interesting email conversations with people from around the world. Her site is used to supplement her hobby, and it provides her with lots of useful contacts, as well as being interesting for other people.

3.1.5 A launchpad site

By 'launchpad site' I mean a site which is particularly concerned with providing lots of links to other websites; I've already mentioned them in fact. If you can provide useful content people will visit you, and return time and time again, allowing you the possibility of attracting them in to look at any other information or material that you've published on the Web. The biggest disadvantage of this type of site, or collection of information is that to be useful it has to be kept up to date, so you will need to spend a considerable portion of your time keeping it current; there are few things worse than links that are out of date.

3.1.6 An Intranet site

An Internet site is outward, looking at the rest of the world. An Intranet site will just be seen by other members of your organisation, and anyone external to the organisation to whom you decide to give access. In many ways, this is perhaps the easiest site of all to create, since you'll know exactly who your audience is, what materials you want to make available and so on. For further information on designing a specific Intranet site I would recommend you take a look at the Aslib Know How guide mentioned in the introduction, *Intranets and push technology*, written by Paul Pedley.

3.2 The audience

Once you've got a clear idea of the type of information you want to make available you have to consider the audience. In fact, you should really be doing this at the same time as you're deciding on content. The audience, or at least your perception of your audience should dramatically affect the design on your site. To give an extreme example, if your audience is perceived as being French, you might decide that it's logical to produce some or all of your pages in French rather than English, or to provide a dual language site.

What sort of keywords will they use to find sites like yours?

Make a list of them, as this will come in useful later on. Will they understand any TLA's (Three Letter Abbreviations) that you might be thinking of using? Will they understand any slang or corporate terms you're used to using? Are they going to just want 'the facts' or will they be interested in ordering information, or having fun at your site?

Where will the audience be coming from?

Once again, this will affect your design style. For example, if you want to attract people from the Third World, they may have slow connections, which means your pages have to load really quickly. On the other hand, they may be UK academics, who don't have access to the latest browsers; sad but true.

What type of connection will they be using?

If you're designing for people with fast connections you can put in many more graphics and other multimedia applications, but if most of your users are going to be using dial-up connections the page, once again, needs to load quickly.

What browser are they likely to be using?

At this stage, you will probably have no idea at all, but this may also affect your design, so you'll need to obtain this information once the site has gone live, and how you do that is covered in Chapter 3, section 3.4.8. You may then discover that 90% of your users connect using a particular browser, and you could decide to design specifically for that browser, especially in the case of an Intranet site.

3.3 Planning the site

By now, you should have spent some considerable time working out the different elements that will go to make up your site, and now you have to start planning the overall look and feel of it. The first thing to get right is the structure of the site; how many pages you have, what they cover and how they link together. An easy way of doing this is to get some standard catalogue cards. On each one, simply write out a suggested title for the page, and jot down some brief ideas as to what the page will contain, a list of keywords and perhaps a 25-word summary for the content of the page.

Once you've done that, you'll have a lot of cards sitting on your table. This is the first physical representation of your entire site. Next, start to arrange the cards in a logical order on the table, then do it again, in a different order! You may find that you can quickly work out a logical sequence of pages; all the departmental pages may be clustered together, or various different product lines may split off from one another for example. You may also find that you need to write out some more cards; one might need to be an overall page to link into the departmental home pages for example. You may realise to your horror that you've missed out a whole section of your organisation, which you only notice when you begin moving the cards around on the table. Hopefully it will now become clear that the time you've spent on this exercise is time well spent; if you'd started by just writing web pages you would then have to go back and start adding more information, with more links, resulting in a site that grows 'like Topsy', rather than having a logical progression to it. Also plan for the future; what if your company decides to branch out into a new area – where would the new pages that mirror this sit in the grand scale of things?

3.4 Planning each individual page

At this stage you're probably champing at the bit to start to write your pages; it's very tempting to launch right in and begin them isn't it? If you really can't wait any longer, skip the rest of this chapter, and move right along to Chapter 5 and begin. However, after you've got over the first rush of enthusiasm, please come back and read the rest of this section, as I'm sure it will affect your design, and if you have to begin again, don't say that I didn't warn you!

Still with me? Good! In this section I want to look at some of the different elements of the page, and the ways in which you can consider including them on each page.

3.4.1 Consistency

The first, and perhaps most important point is to ensure that there is a level of consistency about all the pages that you produce. If you decide to include a logo on each and every page, make sure you position it in exactly the same place. If you're including navigation aids, it makes sense to ensure that they're on the page at exactly the same place, since it will ensure that people can move around the site quickly and smoothly. You'll probably want to try out a few different design styles before settling on the one that you like the best, and the more of a novice you are, the more you'll need to try things out and see what they look like on a page.

Remember that each individual page has to stand on its own merits. You cannot assume that your viewers have visited any other pages on your site, since they may visit a particular page from a link that someone else has created. Therefore, don't be tempted to simply put a 'Back' button at the bottom of the page – tell the viewer where they will be going, such as 'Back to the Information Centre page' or 'Back to the XYZ Company home page'.

3.4.2 The text

You can create a number of different textual effects on the page, such as italicised, emboldened, underlined and even blinking. You can have paragraphs of regular text, block quotations, or pre-formatted (fixed pitch) text. You can put your text into ordered (i.e. items numbered consecutively) or unordered lists. You can change the size of the text, and have it in a variety of different colours (if you really must!). It's also quite possible to align text to the left, right or centre.

Try not to use a lot of different effects in a small space. *It* can <u>make</u> **the text** <u>*quite*</u> $difficult$ *to* read if you do that. (Apologies for that, but it seemed to be the best way of making my point). Choose your default type face and colour and stick with it. Decide how you're going to emphasis particular sections and ensure that you employ the same method(s) throughout the entire site.

3.4.3 The background

Most sites work best with a simple plain background, usually white. This has lots of advantages, since it provides greater clarity and makes it easier if your reader decides to print out a page for use in hard copy. However, you may feel that you want something slightly different, to make either the entire site stand out, or even individual pages. What you chose is of course entirely up to you, but I'd suggest that you take into account readability; it's hard to read black text on a dark blue screen, or red text on a green background for example. Once again, take a look around the Web and see what works well for you. You might decide to have your logo as a background, suitably faded, in grey or embossed. Or you may decide on a simple white background, with a coloured edge running down the left hand side, which is quite popular at the moment.

Try out a variety of different options, and see what they look like. Both on your own computer and any others you can get access to. Monitors are often set up to display colours slightly differently, and just because something works on your screen doesn't necessarily mean it's going to work on anyone else's! Don't forget to also print out the page to make sure that the information is still legible, and try printing it on both a colour printer and a black and white one. You may find you get very different and surprising results!

3.4.4 Graphics

You can of course include graphics on any of your web pages, and they can be very useful. Logos give a level of authority that might otherwise be lacking, so if you have one, I'd certainly commend including it. You might want to also incorporate it into other images, such as a 'back' button for example, or into your background image.

As a general rule of thumb, you should keep your images as small as you possibly can, and by 'small' I mean in terms of the file size, rather than the physical size of the image on the page. The majority of images, such as small flash icons like 'new' or 'updated' should really be no more than 2 or 3k in size. Other images may be rather larger, but again my advice is not to include any image on a page which is more than about 30k in size; it takes a lot longer to download images than text and this may well slow down the loading of the page. If there really is no alternative, include a large image towards the bottom of the page – that way the browser can load the text and your viewer can be reading that while the image continues to load, and by the time they have scrolled down to the bottom of the page the image should have fully downloaded. Perhaps better ideas are to either include a link to an image, such as 'This was a <u>picture</u> of me taken on holiday" or put a small thumbnail image (a much smaller version of the image) on the page, and allow people to click on it if they want to see the full size version. That way you are allowing the viewer to make the choice, rather than forcing it on them.

There are basically two types of image file that you can include on your pages – .gif and .jpg images. GIF images are generally used for small icons, or images with large blocks of colour, while JPG images tend to be photographs. Photographic images are generally the larger of the two, and you may find it worthwhile attempting to reduce the size as much as possible, by using a smaller colour palette for example. You may also find that your graphics package includes an option for reducing the size of images, and if that is the case it is worth using it; it can make the difference between a few seconds wait or a few minutes! If you don't already have access to such a facility, they are available on the Web, either free or for a small fee. Some utilities you might want to look at are listed at http://dir.yahoo.com/Computers_and_Internet/Software/Graphics/Titles/

If you are saving an image as a GIF file, you have two further options available to you. You can choose to interlace the image, and provide a transparent background. You'll have seen interlaced images, even if you didn't realise that is what they were, if you've seen an image that starts off very 'blocky' but slowly sharpens up in a series of waves. Alternatively images will be displayed in their final version, but will appear on the screen in lines, or you will have to wait for the entire image to be downloaded onto the computer hard disk before it is displayed. My preference is to use an interlaced image when possible, so the viewer knows that something is happening, and they can choose to wait for the entire image to download if they like the look of it, or they can simply move on. Transparent backgrounds can also help turn an amateur-looking page into a professional one very quickly. Each image that you create is contained either within a square, or an oblong. Although you might consider the image to be the picture, the background is also just as much a part of the image, and if you don't have a transparent background you will see not only the image, but the rest of the square or block. By choosing a transparent background the only part of the image you see is the part that you expect to. The best way of illustrating this is to give you an example, and figures 1 and 2 show a hand without a transparent background and with one.

Figure 1 – a non transparent background

Figure 2 – a transparent background

You can, I hope, see quite clearly what a difference it makes! Both the interlacing and transparent background effects can be produced by the majority of graphics packages these days.

Two final points to mention with the use of graphics are: to include information in your HTML coding to give both an alternative text version of the graphic, and to put in a height and width attribute. You'll see exactly how to do that in Chapter 5 but I'll explain why you want to do that here. If you don't put in alternative text, if someone is browsing the Web with their graphics turned off they won't have any idea as to what your images are. If alternative text is included, they'll see a small message (written by you) which says something like 'Logo' or 'Campus map', thus allowing them the opportunity of turning graphics back on to view the image. Height and width are important because they allow the browser to block out a certain amount of space on the page that the image will fit into and it can start to download the image at the same time as getting more text. This means that your audience can continue to read the text while the image is downloading. If you do not include these attributes the browser has to stop at that point to download the image and place it on the screen. Only when it has done that is it in a position to work out where the rest of the text goes, which slows up the whole process.

If you've never experimented, you might like to browse the Web for a while with your graphics turned off, in order to see how useful alternative text can be, or how irritating you'll find it if that's not been included.

3.4.5 Frames

The majority of Web pages do not make use of frames; they are an entity in their own right, and if you scroll down the page, the entire page moves with the scroll bar. However, you will come across sites that do make use of frames. A frames page has a number of different elements on it, which work independently of each other, so you might have a menu of choices in a left-hand frame, and when you click on an item, a new page is loaded into the body of the screen, while leaving the menu options untouched. You will then be able to scroll through both parts of the screen independently of each other. Frames pages can be a very useful navigation tool, allowing you to always ensure that certain information (usually links or icons to other pages on the site) is constantly available in exactly the same place.

However, in many cases (and I'll admit a certain bias here as I don't like them) they act only to clutter up a page unnecessarily and if badly implemented cause confusion for the viewer. More importantly, some search engines are unable to follow frames pages when they try and index a site (and I'll talk more about frames in Chapter 9) which will reduce the possibility of your site being found when people run searches.

I demonstrate how to include frames on your pages later, in Chapter 9 but I would caution you to think quite hard about them; unless they really do add to a site they may be better left unimplemented.

3.4.6 JavaScript

It is outside the scope of this title to go into great detail about JavaScript, since it requires a particular level of skill to include it on a site; in any but the most simple applications it does help if you have some programming knowledge or background. However, JavaScript applets can allow you to do some interesting things to your web pages, and I've included some sample JavaScript coding that you might want to include for yourself, once you become more confident in authoring pages.

3.4.7 Forms

Forms allow you to provide a greater level of interaction with your site, and if you want to encourage people to send you information (other than a simple email) you may wish to include them. They can be as simple or as complex as you wish and can include text, checkboxes, radio buttons, hidden fields or passworded fields.

You may also choose to produce menus to allow the user to choose from a list of options that you provide, which can be quite useful if for example you have a number of products available. The users can then simply choose the options that interest them.

3.4.8 Access counters

Every web author wants to see how many people have visited their site; it's human nature. It can also be useful to ensure that your site is active and useful, if you can see how many visitors you have had. There are essentially two ways that you have of finding out this sort of information, the first being an access counter on your web page. These are not difficult to produce, and indeed there are many websites that will provide you with such a utility if it's not readily available on the server you host your pages with. (I'll talk about this in more detail in Chapter 12). Generally, I don't encourage the use of them on 'professional' pages, since they can look a little tacky, although I admit this is a personal bias, even if I do have one on my own site! If you want to obtain information on the number of visitors to your site you may be better off using an access analyser which sits on the server and keeps details of all your visitors. Access analysers can provide you with a host of information, such as:

- total number of visitors
- geographical location of visitors
- number of accesses to particular pages
- most frequent visitors

- the browsers used to access your site
- most popular times of day, day of the week
- where people came from to visit your site

and so on.

Every time someone visits your site, their browser will pass some information onto your server, and this data will be stored in a statistics file, for later manipulation. It's a much neater way of obtaining data on the number of visitors you have had, and a good analyser will provide you with much more data than a simple counter. More information on these utilities can be found at http://dir.yahoo.com/Business_and_Economy/Companies/Computers/Business_to_Business/Software/Internet/World_Wide_Web/Log_Analysis_Tools/Titles/

3.4.9 Mailto: forms

As well as finding out who is coming to your page, you can use a mailto: form to allow visitors to send you email. At its simplest level it allows the user to connect back to their preferred email package and send you a message. Not only is this useful, but it also provides a level of re-assurance; if someone is prepared to accept email messages, it's reasonable to assume that they are taking good care of the page, otherwise they are opening themselves up to the possibility that people will quickly send them an email telling them what's wrong with it!

3.4.10 Links

Few Web pages stand entirely on their own merits. While people may be able to locate your page by using one of the standard search engines, many more people will find your pages (and navigate around your site) because they have followed a particular link.

You should therefore consider linking your pages to those of others. If you have a commercial website you might want to link to a professional body that covers your subject area, or perhaps to other organisations that work in the same field. If you are running a Web site for an academic organisation you might want to link to other academic sites and so on.

Also consider how your page can be of benefit to your readers, and we have already looked at how a launchpad site can assist them, and encourage them to come back to you on a regular basis.

Although having a link that leaves your site doesn't initially help in getting people to come to it, it never hurts to send an email to the web author of the site or page that you're considering linking to, since there is an underlying hint that it might be nice if they made a link back to you! Technically, as we shall see, it's very easy indeed to make a link to another site. You don't really even require permission from the site owner to do this, although it's a slightly grey area at the moment, and there have been one or two cases that have gone through the legal system which imply that getting express permission to link is a good idea. You may sometimes find that the author of a site prefers links to go directly to their home page, rather than to any others on their site, and if they request this, it makes sense to comply with this request, or you'll lose the opportunity of getting them to link back to you.

Of course, the opposite also applies. As you can link to other people, they can link to you, and you may not even be aware of this. You can however discover this by visiting a search engine and doing a search for exactly that. AltaVista for example has an option called 'link:'. In order to see who has linked to you, simply visit that search engine and type:

link:www.mysite.com

and you will see all of the links that other people have made to you. It also shows any links that your pages make to each other, so to eliminate these you could instead try:

+link:www.mysite.com −host:www.mysite.com

which will exclude your own site from the results returned to you.

If you're unhappy with any links that come into your site you can of course email the site owner and request that the link is removed, or you may wish to have a disclaimer on your site which states that you don't necessarily endorse any organisation that has linked to you.

A final word of caution regarding this business of linking to other sites. In most cases you will not be able to control the data on the third party site (unless it's a sister organisation, or part of your own organisation for example), so you will have to check to make sure the links work on a regular basis – it's quite possible that the author of the page you're linking to might take it down. Alternatively, and worse, you may find that the site has been taken over by another organisation, and the content has changed. There was a case earlier this year when one well-respected site was re-registered to a pornographic company, and as a result one Monday morning just about every British University found themselves linking to a hard core pornography site! As a result, you may also wish to have a disclaimer stating that you have no control over the content of third party sites.

3.4.11 Page length

Unlike hard copy material, where you have a limit on the amount of space available, the space available to your site is, to all intents and purposes, infinite. You may therefore find it tempting to consider just creating one huge page, which acts as a home page and everything else as well. There are very good reasons why you shouldn't do this.

Firstly, a long page can take a lot of time to load. Viewers can also find it difficult to find their way around it, and printing it out becomes impossible. Moreover you will find it almost impossible to get a high ranking with different search engines, for reasons discussed in the next chapter.

When you've finished your page, print it out. If it's longer than 4 A4 pages in length in my opinion it's too long. If it's less than half an A4 page, it's too short. Consider splitting the page into two or more pages, with links between them, or adding in more information. There are of course exceptions to this rule; many of the pages on my site for example are ten or twelve pages long, but they are articles which are designed to be printed out and used on courses that I run. So perhaps I should qualify my earlier statement by saying that in most cases keep your pages within the half A4 - 4A4 page limit, depending on the purpose of the page!

4. Working with the search engines

As I've previously mentioned, you'll need to make sure that, as much as possible, you get a good ranking with the search engines; there is little point in having an excellent page if no-one can find it! In this chapter I'd like to briefly discuss some of the ways in which you can ensure that you maximise your chances of getting that good rating, rather than finding yourself as one of the also-rans. Given the scope of this title I'm not going to go into great detail, but will limit myself to some key pointers, and would direct you to another Aslib Know How guide *How to promote your web site effectively*, written by Mark Kerr, for more information.

As an end user, I suspect that you've used search engines to find appropriate information, and have sometimes been puzzled about which pages turn up as a result of your searches, and which ones don't. As an end user it doesn't really matter that much, as long as you get the information you require, but as a web author it may be quite crucial that the search engines list your page in a high position; this is another difference that you'll have discovered between end users of web pages and authors of web pages.

There are of course, many different search engines available on the Internet, and I've seen figures which range from between 3,000 to 15,000 engines.

However, before you start to worry, you can ignore the majority of them; for our purposes we only need be concerned with the major search engines, such as AltaVista, HotBot, FAST, Yahoo! and so on. There are two major types of engine that web authors need concern themselves with, and those are free text engines, such as the aforementioned AltaVista, and index or directory based engines, such as Yahoo!

Free text engines create their indexes by 'spidering' sites; that is, following links from page to page, and once they find a new page, or a page that's been updated since the last time they visited, they copy the data on the page back to base and include it in a newly created index. So when you run a search, you're actually searching their indexes. In many cases you'll get thousands, if not millions of results, and these results are then placed into a relevance ranked order for you to view them.

Consequently, as much as possible you need to ensure that your page is going to be ranked highly, by ensuring that the search engines realise that your page is particularly relevant to relation to the search that's been done. There are a number of ways you can go about this, some of them perfectly acceptable, others less so, and if you're caught employing dubious techniques you may find that your pages, or your entire site are deleted from the search engine database. So it's important that you get this right!

Every one of the search engines that employ a ranking system uses a series of algorithms to work out which web pages are more relevant than others, but since this is one of their key selling points (we give better results than our competitors) it is understandable, but unfortunate, that they're not keen on explaining these in detail. Therefore, it's necessary for web authors to try and work these out for themselves. As a result, I can't really talk about how specific search engines use particular algorithms, partly because I don't know, and partly because they change them on a regular basis. All I can suggest here is that if you want to get a good ranking with a particular search engine, run some searches and see which pages come at the top of the listings, and take a close look at them. You should be able to get a fairly clear idea of exactly how the engine ranks, and you can then write your pages accordingly.

However, some of the points to bear in mind are:

URL

Some more sophisticated search engines will take the URL into account. (Just to remind you, the URL is the address of the web page, such as http:// www.philb.com/html/guide.htm) You may get a better ranking if you can include any keywords here, either as a sub-directory, or the name of a particular file. We'll see how to do this slightly later.

Title

This is important for two reasons. Firstly, some search engines will pay particular attention to terms that they find in the title element of the web page. It is therefore very important to choose a title which clearly reflects the content of the page. Secondly, when a user bookmarks or uses the favourites option, the default used by the browsers is to take information from the title element. Consequently a title such as 'My home page' or 'Widgets Incorporated' isn't going to be that helpful in either instance. Better examples would be 'Phil Bradley's Home Page' or 'Widgets Incorporated – Annual Report'.

Use of the <H1> element.

We'll look in detail at this later, but to put it into context for you, it's the HTML tag which gives a very large font size on the screen. If the search engine can find key words within this element on the page it will be given greater priority than simply finding the same words in the body of the text.

First 25 words

This again is important for two reasons. The first is that some search engines will only index using the first few words; some will go up to 50 or 100 words, but I always try to concentrate on the first 25 words. The second reason is that many search engines will use the first 25 words to create the summary information you find below the URL in returned hits. This is the reason why I suggested in the planning stage that you create a 25 word summary for the document, and this should become the opening paragraph. For a page that is directed at information professionals you might want to consider something such as:

"Librarians, information professionals and library workers will find this site helpful when creating web pages; it is a beginner's guide to writing good library pages".

You'll notice that I've chosen as key words 'librarians' 'information professionals' 'library' (twice), the phrases 'beginner's guide' and 'creating web pages' – all terms that I could reasonably expect someone to use when doing a search in this subject area. I've also used a few synonyms for 'librarian'; this may be important or not, depending on the content of your pages, and also don't forget American English spellings either!

Repetition

You may find that some engines will rank a page more highly if keywords are used several times; a web page that uses 'widgets' seven times may well get a higher ranking than one that uses 'widgets' once. However, you do need to be careful with this, since if you mention key words too often, the search engines may consider that you're trying to 'spam' them (fool them), so don't be tempted to have a page that has text such as 'widgets, widgets, widgets, widgets, widgets'. Not only does it look silly and is unreadable, it won't work. What works better is to ensure that you slip key words into the page as appropriate, so pay attention to them, but not too much attention! Some engines will also take into account the total number of words on a page and will work out the overall percentage of words in relation to each other, so a shorter page with 'widgets' in five times might well be more effective than a much longer page that uses 'widgets' seven times.

Proximity

Two keywords near each other may be more effective than the same words spread throughout the page. You may find that 'beginner's guide' will work better than 'Beginners will find this a useful guide to...'

Links

When first published, your pages won't have many links coming into them. Hopefully however you will have produced an excellent page that lots of people want to link to, and some search engines will take into account the number of links coming into your site and will give higher rankings to those sites with more links. Over the course of time you may therefore find that your pages move up an index as more people link to them.

Meta tags

Meta tags are a particularly crucial area, since most of the search engines will pay very particular attention to them. I expect that most of the other items listed above will not come as that much of a surprise to you, since they are reasonably logical. However, unless you've spent a lot of time looking at the source code for pages you won't have come across these before, since they don't actually appear on the web page itself, but remain hidden, and are really only used by search engines. I'll talk in much more detail later on about these tags, but there are two important ones that I need to mention in the context of good rankings. The first of these is the Keyword tag. It is here that you should put all those keywords that you listed at the planning stage. I would suggest limiting yourself to a maximum of 1,024 characters, so be selective, and put them into this element in descending order of importance. Each keyword should be separated by a comma and a space, though if you're using a phrase, just use a comma at the very end of the phrase. To take my example a little further, I'd probably use a set of keywords such as:

librarians, librarian, information professional, library, libraries

and so on, if I particularly wanted to emphasise just how important my page was to the information community (and there's another phrase I could have used!) Keywords can also prove useful if there are words which you know are important, but for some reason it's not appropriate to put them into the body of the page, such as American spellings.

The second important meta tag is the Description. This is basically the same as using the 25-word introductory paragraph as mentioned above. If it's really not practical to do that on your Web page, it can be placed in the Description element instead. If you can use the first 25 words to good effect on the page, put them into this element as well! Since I think Meta tags are so important I've dedicated the whole of Chapter 11 to them.

Checking your ranking

Once you've got your page(s) on the web and registered with the search engines (and just how you do that is covered in Chapter 12), you'll need to check to see how well you've managed to get high rankings. As you've probably worked out for yourself, this whole process is not an exact science, by any means! There are a number of different Web based utilities that you can use to check your position, such as Position Agent at http:// www.positionagent.com/ and it's worth using them to see how well you've done. I'd suggest waiting for a few days before doing this though, just to make sure that your page(s) have been indexed before you try this out – don't do it immediately after you've registered, because you'll get a negative result. When you do check your ranking though, hopefully you'll find that you're in the top ten for your particular keywords, but if not, take a look at those pages that are, work out why, and try and do the same thing yourself, and re-submit your pages.

You should also check your position on a regular basis, since everyone else is also trying to do exactly the same thing, and some of them may be more successful than you are!

Other search engines

Index or Directory-based search engines work rather differently. A good example of this type is Yahoo! which uses a hierarchical approach, with major headings, sub-headings under those and so on. You should look through the headings until you find an appropriate place for your page/site and click on the 'Add URL' button at that point. Please make sure that you chose the correct sub-heading, since more registration requests fail through choosing an incorrect heading than anything else.

Importing pages from elsewhere

There is no reason at all why you shouldn't use previously created material such as word processed files for inclusion in web pages, either by cut and paste or by importing them directly into an authoring tool (covered in Chapter 13). However, if you do this, please remember that to get good rankings, based on the above information you may well need to alter the text, sometimes substantially in order to meet the criteria set by the searching engines to give such data a good ranking.

5. Writing Web pages

We've finally reached the section of the book where I actually start to talk about how you write your Web pages. I make no apology for leaving it until this point, for the simple reason that anyone can put a Web site together – it's not actually that difficult. What is difficult however is designing a good site; one that is ranked highly by the search engines, is quick to load and easy to navigate. If you've followed all the steps in the previous sections you'll now have a lot of ideas and clear indications of what information you want to put where. In this section of the book we'll look at how you actually go about translating all those ideas into a web page.

As already mentioned, this is done by using HTML, which is a series of tags or instructions, that the browser understands. HTML is not a page design language; it was not meant for screen-based desktop publishing. It describes how the information on a page is organised, rather like an outliner program. It is up to the user to decide exactly how the page looks on their screen, since they can set their own options in their browser, such as choosing whether to auto-load images for example. HTML is intended to convey information in a consistent format readable by as many applications as possible. Information on hypertext pages will often be searched for and indexed by other software packages prior to being read by human beings (the spider programs used by search engines for example), and these programs are not interested in how a page looks, only if it contains the text that they have been asked to find.

HTML commands are passed onto the browser in the form of tags which are inserted before and usually after text. They describe and instruct the browser on how to display text, images and so on. For example:

```
<STRONG> This line will typically appear to
be in bold type </STRONG>
```

The <STRONG> . . . </STRONG> phrase mark-up tags delimit the text you want to appear as bold. Note that each tag is wrapped in the < and > signs. This tells the browser that when it finds these characters they start or end a command. I'll be using upper case in the HTML pages, but this is not a requirement, since the important thing is the < and >, but it will make it easier for you to see what is an HTML tag and what isn't. When you're writing your pages, decide for yourself which you prefer, but be consistent, since it will make your life a lot easier in the long run!

Tools of the trade

You'll only need two simple software tools to construct a basic page or site – a text editor or word processor (more sophisticated or recent word processing applications now offer to save data in an HTML format, but for our purposes, save any files you create in plain ASCII format only), and if you want to include graphics, an application that can save graphics as GIF files, which most of them can.

You really don't need anything more than that! Of course, you'll probably want to use an 'authoring tool'; a software package specifically designed to write HTML for you, and I think that's a good idea – it's certainly the way that I write all of my pages. I've included more details on such packages in Chapter 13 and I would encourage you to try some out until you find one that you like. However, it's useful to learn 'raw' HTML (that is, writing it for yourself in a text editor), since it will give you a much better background in and understanding of how it works. It will also mean that when you look at the code someone else has produced it will make much more sense to you.

So, settle yourself down at your computer with this book by your side (coffee is a suggested extra but isn't required), and fire up your word processor, or the Windows text editor Notepad if you prefer. To keep things simple you might want to save your page onto a floppy disk, or alternatively, create a folder called 'web pages' or similar to store your work in.

An example home page

There are several basic things that you must include in your HTML script, and in a particular order – they tell the browser that it is supposed to display a Web page, and the name under which the page should be indexed.

In the following examples, the HTML tags are all in upper case, as previously mentioned, and the font I'm using is Courier New simply to make a clear distinction between what is on the page and my comments. You don't need to do the same, I'm just doing this to make it easier to follow.

Simply type the following (or make up your own text) into your text editor:

```
<HTML>
<HEAD>
<TITLE>The librarian's guide to HTML </TITLE>
</HEAD>
<BODY>
</BODY>
</HTML>
```

Next, save this file onto your floppy or into your folder and call the file index.htm

I'll save my explanation of what all of the above means for a moment, because I know you want to see what you've created. So open up your browser (I'm using Netscape for my examples, but any other browser will do exactly the same job) and point it to the page that you've just created. What you should see on the screen is something very similar to figure 3 below.

Don't panic because you don't see very much on the screen – at this stage you're not supposed to! All that should be there is the title of the page in the browser title bar (The librarian's guide to HTML) and the location of the file in the Location bar in the browser.

Now that you've had a look at what you created, let's see just how you created it.

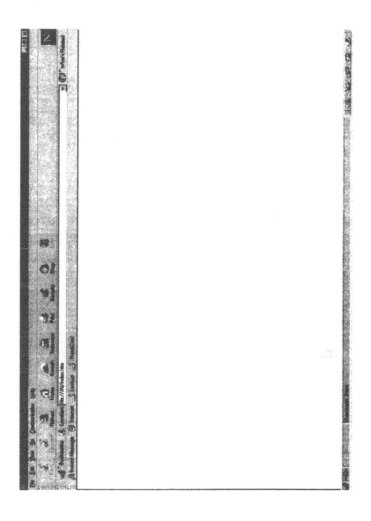

Figure 3

<HTML>
This tells the browser that everything that follows is to be regarded as a hypertext document.

<HEAD>
Opens the HEAD element, which contains information that describes the page. Indexing and search applications look here and return what they find; this is also where we'll put the Meta tag information a little later.

<TITLE>. . . </TITLE>
The text between the opening and closing element is what the browser and search engines will see as the title to the page. Also note that this is first of the closing tags, and the / followed by the tag tells the browser that particular instruction (in this case the title element) is now over.

</HEAD>
Another closing tag, which closes the HEAD element.

<BODY> . . . </BODY>
Between these tags is where you'll put the text, pictures and anything else that you want people to read.

</HTML>
This tells the browser that the hypertext document finishes at this point.

Having created the basics of the page, we can now start to do something a little bit more interesting.

```
<HTML>
<HEAD>
<TITLE>The librarian's guide to HTML </TITLE>
</HEAD>
```

```
<BODY>
<H1>Welcome to The Librarian's guide to HTML
web site! </H1>
</BODY>
</HTML>
```

Save the file once again, and then display it. You should get something that looks like figure 4 below:

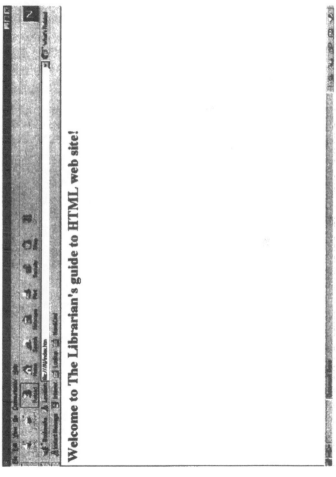

Figure 4

<H1>. . . </H1>

These tags indicate headings ranging from H1 (top level) down to H6. They fulfil the role of section headings. Each browser sets its own defaults for displaying them (which are user configurable). Experiment with your browser and see what they are. Headings will typically include space above and below and the heading line will automatically break after the closing tag. If you want to experiment a little and see the different effects that you get by changing the H1 header to one of the others, please do, but remember you need to change the instruction in both the opening and closing tag; if you don't the browser will get confused and may not display your text correctly.

I'll start to add some more information into the page, so you can see the effects the different tags have, and once again I'll explain what I've done afterwards.

```
<HTML>
<HEAD>
<TITLE>The librarian's guide to HTML </TITLE>
</HEAD>
<BODY>
<H1>Welcome to The Librarian's guide to HTML
web site! </H1>
<P>Librarians, information professionals,
library workers will all find something
interesting on this site, since it explains
how to write HTML code. </P>
<H2>What you'll find in on this site </H2>
<P ALIGN="center"> Examples of code, sources
of further information, and lots of other
useful material. It will be of particular use
to <B>novices</B> </P>
</BODY>
</HTML>
```

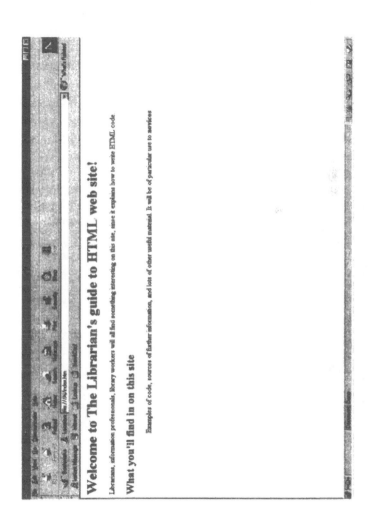

Figure 5

<H2> . . . </H2>
This is a second level heading, which you might already have discovered if you've been experimenting.

<P> . . . </P>
This is the paragraph element. If you want to start a new paragraph, simply end one with the closing tag and start a new one. With most browsers this will automatically insert a space between both paragraphs. If you want to break a paragraph, by stopping in the middle of one line and starting again one line down you can use the break, or <BR> element immediately after the word after which you want the line to break. There is no closing tag to this element, since it is a command that tells the browser to execute one very specific instruction.

If we look at the HTML coding we've already done, you'll notice that in most cases I've started each one on a new line. This is simply to make it easier to see on the page. The browser doesn't actually care if I start everything on new lines; in fact it would be quite happy if I wrote all the code on a single line! All it is interested in are instructions, so it's looking for angled brackets and tags within them. If you start a new line in your text editor just by pressing the return key it may look to you as though you've started a new line, or a new paragraph, but the browser will simply ignore it. It will only start a new line on the screen, or a new paragraph, if you include the appropriate tag. (The exception to this is however that the browser knows how big the window is, and it will automatically perform a wrap-round for a long sentence or paragraph; you do not need to worry about that.)

<P ALIGN="center"> . . . *</P>*
This time, instead of writing a straightforward paragraph, I decided to centre it. Note the US English spelling of centre as well. The attributes are 'left' (the default), 'center', 'right' and 'justify'. You must include the closing </P> tag if you use paragraph attributes, but I'd suggest always including it anyway, since it is good practice.

<B> . . .*</B>*
This is an instruction to tell the browser to display text as emboldened on the screen, and once again, the browser will do this according to its own defaults. You might want to also try <I> ...</I> which will give you italics on the screen. If you want to combine both bold and italics, simply place one set of tags inside the other; it doesn't matter which way you do this, but they have to nest properly, so correct HTML would be:

```
<B><I>Some text</I></B>
```

but

```
<B><I>Some text</B></I>
```

would be incorrect, as the tags don't nest properly. Some versions of some browsers will be able to cope with broken code like this, but others may have problems, so it's as well to get it right in the first place!

Adding graphics

Adding in text, and playing around with it is all well and good, but after a while you're going to want to add in something visually eye-catching, which of course means graphics. Before you can do this, you'll need to find your graphic. Many graphics packages will have sample graphics that you can use, or you might just want to use such a package to create your own. If you're a poor graphic artist (as I am), you'll probably decide against creating your own, at least to begin with. There are lots of graphics libraries available on the Web, such as http://dir.yahoo.com/Arts/ Design_Arts/Graphic_Design/ Web_Page_Design_and_Layout/Graphics/ which offers links to many useful sites, some of which include public domain images, which you will be free to copy and use on your own pages. You might see a nice graphic while you're browsing the Web, but please don't take it and use it yourself without permission from the author of the site, since it may not be a public domain image and you could find yourself infringing copyright legislation. If in doubt ask; if really in doubt, find something else instead.

Once you've found or created your graphic, save it into the same directory as your file. The main reason for doing this is to make things easier at this early stage, although later on we'll want to make things a little tidier by moving graphics into their own sub-directories.

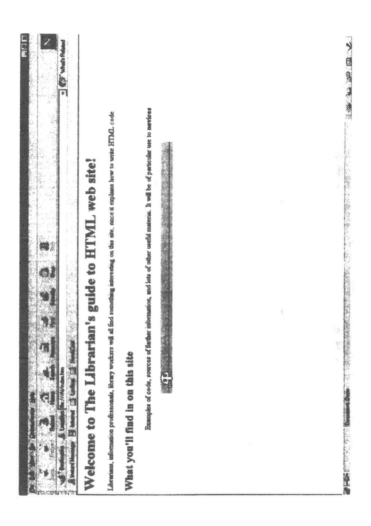

Figure 6

```
<HTML>
<HEAD>
<TITLE>The librarian's guide to HTML </TITLE>
</HEAD><BODY>
<H1>Welcome to The Librarian's guide to HTML
web site! </H1>
<P>Librarians, information professionals,
library workers will all find something
interesting on this site, since it explains
how to write HTML code. </P>
<H2>What you'll find in on this site </H2>
<P ALIGN="center"> Examples of code, sources
of further information, and lots of other
useful material. It will be of particular use
to <B>novices</B> </P>
<CENTER><IMG SRC="kilroy.gif" ALT="Horizontal
Line" WIDTH="560" HEIGHT="26"></CENTER>
</BODY>
</HTML>
```

<CENTER> . . . </CENTER>

The center tag will centre anything between the opening and closing tags, such as text, images or tables for example.

<IMG SRC="kilroy.gif"

This tag specifies the image source that the browser will use to display the image on the screen. An important point to make here is that you need to be very careful when naming the image file, paying particularly close attention to upper or lower case. In a Windows environment there is no distinction between upper and lower case file names, but when you upload your finished web page (plus graphics files) onto the server in all probability you'll be uploading to a UNIX based system which does make a difference, and it will mean that if you have referenced your image as Kilroy.gif, but the actual filename is kilroy.gif (all in lower case) the browser won't be able to display the image file on the page. If that doesn't make too much sense at this point, don't worry about it, just stay consistent, and ensure that all your images are saved in (for example) lower case, and that you reference them that way in the <IMG SRC . . . > tag.

You'll also notice that there doesn't appear to be a closing tag, in the way that we've previously seen. This is because we're dealing with a discreet unit of information; it's just an image, so the browser doesn't need to be told to stop putting the image on the screen.

ALT="Horizontal Line"
This is the alternative text for the image, as previously mentioned, so if people have their images turned off, they'll simply see a box which is the size of the image, with the words 'Horizontal Line' inside it. You'll also notice that the tag doesn't have an angled bracket at the start either; this is taken care of by the opening one for the <IMG SRC . . . > tag. It does however contain double quote marks, because the text we've used is a variable, and all variables are indicated by the use of the double quote marks.

WIDTH="560" HEIGHT="26">
Both of these should make sense to you; the numbers indicate the size of the image by number of pixels. If you're not sure how large the image is, your graphics package should have an option which tells you this. Finally we have a closing angled bracket to indicate to the browser that we've finished that particular command.

Incidentally, my graphic was used to split the page in two, but the same effect can be used with a Horizontal Rule <HR> which is used on its own, with no closing tag.

Adding links

I think at this point I can stop copying the entire HTML code for you, since I'm sure you've got the idea behind it now. When I add in new tags I'll simply annotate them without repeating everything – besides, it will be easier to identify the new tags without having to hunt through the entire document. I'll also just include screen shots of the appropriate part of the screen as well, as with Figure 7.

```
<P><A HREF="http://www.philb.com">Phil
Bradley's site</A>

has lots of articles that you might find
useful as a starting point. <BR>

Another useful site is <A HREF="http://
amazon.co.uk">the Amazon Bookshop</A>

which will be happy to sell other books on
the subject.</P>

<A HREF="http://www.philb.com">Phil Bradley's
site</A>
```

The <A HREF= . . .> is an anchor, telling the browser that there is a link to somewhere else; either on that page, or to another page on the same site, or indeed, with the example we have here, to a different site entirely, in this case mine! As you can see, first of all you need to tell the browser where the link is going to, and the text immediately after that

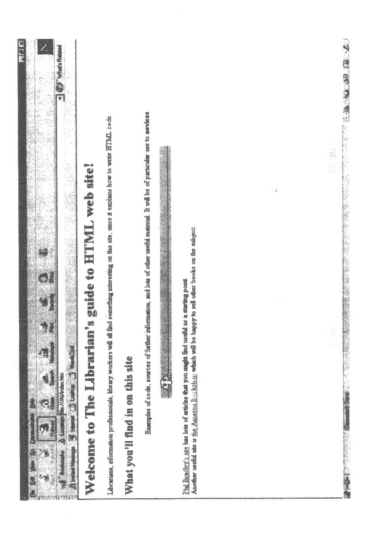

Figure 7

is the actual link that will be displayed on the screen, usually as blue underlined text. Clicking once on an anchor will send the browser to find and display the file or page specified in the link, so you can make the text say anything you want it to.

If you want to, there is no reason why you shouldn't use an image instead, or as well as a text link. To do that you need your image, which needs to be placed into the <A> . . . </A> tag. So you could include an icon with the Amazon link for example, and it would look something like this:

```
<A HREF="http://www.amazon.co.uk"><IMG
SRC="books.gif" ALT="Link to Amazon"
HEIGHT="50" WIDTH="50">Amazon Bookshop</A>
```

Lists

Looking at the example used above, and particularly the screen shot, you might decide that the links would look better as bullet points instead. There are two ways that this can be achieved, which is to use Ordered or Unordered lists. The difference is simple; Ordered lists follow a 1,2,3, while unordered lists simply have a small bullet point next to them. You don't need to put either the numbers or the small bullet point icon in; the browser will automatically do that for you. So, if we make a slight change to the links, we'll see how this works in Figure 8.

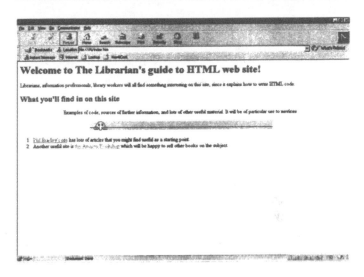

Figure 8

```
<OL>
<LI><A HREF="http://www.philb.com">Phil
Bradley's site</A> has lots of articles that
you might find useful as a starting point
<LI>Another useful site is <A HREF="http://
amazon.co.uk">the Amazon Bookshop</A> which
will be happy to sell other books on the
subject.
</OL>
```

<OL> . . . </OL>

This is the tag for an Ordered List, and all of the items included sit inside the opening and closing tags.

<LI>

This indicates each item in the list. There is no closing tag.

`<UL> ... </UL>`
This tag obviously isn't included in the example above, but if you decide you want bullets rather than numbers, simply replace the `<OL> ... </OL>` with these instead.

Another way of displaying a list is to use tags for Definition Terms `<DT>` and Definition Data `<DD>`.This will typically display with the Definition term left aligned and the Definition Data formatted as an indented paragraph immediately below it. You can try this for yourself by inserting the `<DT>` tag immediately in front of the Anchor tab in the above example (having deleted the Ordered list and List Item tags!) and the `<DT>` tag at the end of the anchor tag with some text. Neither tag requires closing.

Mail to:
This is another useful tag, and one that you should hopefully include on almost every page that you write. It will allow people to send you email, if their browser has been configured to work with an email package. It's another tag that makes use of the Anchor link and looks like this:

```
<A HREF="mailto:philb@philb.com"> Send Phil
an email!</A>
```

6. Forms

Forms are another integral part of a Web page. One of the major advantages of a Web page is that, as well as displaying information to your viewers, it can provide you with feedback, such as by mailing comments to you, but can also provide you with other information as well. For example, you can provide viewers with a page in which they can fill out an order form to purchase or order products. This section deals with one of the several ways in which this can be made possible. Figure 9 shows the form we'll create.

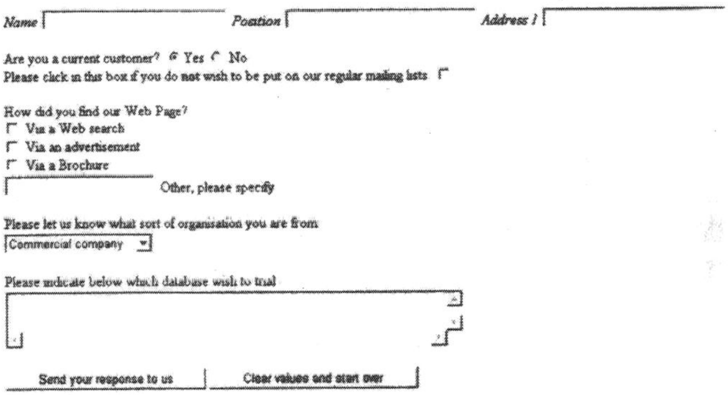

Figure 9

```
<FORM ACTION="mailto:philb@philb.com"
METHOD="POST" ENCTYPE="text/plain">
<I>Name</I>
<INPUT NAME="Name" SIZE="25" MAXLENGTH="50">
<I>Position</I>
<INPUT NAME="Position" SIZE="25"
```

```
MAXLENGTH="50">
<I>Address 1</I>
<INPUT TYPE="TEXT" NAME="Address1" SIZE="25">

<P>Are you a current customer?:
<INPUT TYPE="RADIO" NAME="Customer"
VALUE="Yes" CHECKED="CHECKED">Yes
<INPUT TYPE="RADIO" NAME="Customer"
VALUE="No"> No
<BR>
Please click in this box if you do <B>not</B>
wish to be put on our regular mailing lists.
<INPUT TYPE="CHECKBOX" NAME="Not on mailing
list" VALUE="Not on mailing list">
</P>

<P>How did you find our Web Page?
<BR>
<INPUT TYPE="CHECKBOX" NAME="Find - web"> Via
a Web search
<BR>
<INPUT TYPE="CHECKBOX" NAME="Find - advert">
Via an advertisement
<BR>
<INPUT TYPE="CHECKBOX" NAME="Find - Bro-
chure"> Via a Brochure
<BR>
<INPUT TYPE="TEXT" NAME="Find - other">
Other, please specify</P>

<P>Please let us know what sort of organisa-
tion you are from:<BR>
<SELECT NAME="Location">
<OPTION>Commercial company</OPTION>
<OPTION>Academic organisation</OPTION>
<OPTION>Individual</OPTION>
</OPTION>
</SELECT>
</P>

<P>Please indicate below which database wish
to trial
<BR>
<TEXTAREA NAME="Trial request for:" ROWS="2"
COLS="60"></TEXTAREA>
</P>
```

```
<P><INPUT TYPE="SUBMIT" VALUE="Send your
response to us">
<INPUT TYPE="RESET" VALUE="Clear values and
start over"></P>
</FORM>
```

(Obviously, this form would be included as part of a web page; in fact it's based on a form that I produced for a client, so you'll have to image the rest of the tags in place around the form such as the <BODY> . . . </BODY> tags for example).

<FORM ACTION="mailto:philb@philb.com" METHOD="POST" ENCTYPE="text/plain">
When someone fills out a form they will have to be able to send it back to you, so this is what this tag takes care of. The action element specifies what is to happen to the form when completed, and the method element specifies how the information is sent to the server. There are two possible options here; GET and POST. The first appends the data to the URL, but the one we're using sends the information as a separate email. The ENCTYPE="text/plain"> ensures that the data is sent to you as a plain text file; if you don't include this all the different fields that are filled in by the user will still be sent back to you, but as a single string, which is difficult to read.

<INPUT NAME="Name" SIZE="25" MAXLENGTH="50">
This tag allows you to specify a text box, with the size as it appears on the screen (25 characters long), and a maximum length (50 characters). The name element ensures that when you are sent the form you can see exactly which field refers to which field

as filled in. Consequently the data that would be returned to you from this particular element (in the email) would look like this:

Name=Joe Bloggs

```
<INPUT TYPE="RADIO" NAME="Customer"
VALUE="Yes" CHECKED="CHECKED">Yes
<INPUT TYPE="RADIO" NAME="Customer"
VALUE="No"> No
```

Radio buttons are useful if you want to give your respondent a single choice from a variety of options, in this case if they are an existing customer or not. Please note that when using a radio button, the variable NAME="Customer" must be the same in each option. As a result, in the returned form this section might look like this:

Customer=No

```
<INPUT TYPE="CHECKBOX" NAME="Find - web"> Via
a Web search
```

Checkboxes are useful if you want your respondent to be able to choose any number of options. In this particular example, the returned form would look something like:

Find – web Yes

(obviously if that option had been ticked).

```
<SELECT NAME="Location">
<OPTION>Commercial company</OPTION>
<OPTION>Academic organisation</OPTION>
<OPTION>Individual</OPTION>
</OPTION>
</SELECT>
```

There may well be times when you have so many options that someone might chose, it makes more sense to have the options in a pull down menu. Although I obviously can't show this option in operation in a print form, the respondent will be able to click on the box (as seen in figure 9 above) and a pull down menu will appear, allowing them to choose the option that is appropriate for them. You'll see this option yourself when filling out forms on Web pages, particularly when you have to choose a particular country of origin for example. Once again, in the returned form the result would look like:

Location=Commercial company

<TEXTAREA NAME="Trial request for:"
ROWS="2" COLS="60"></TEXTAREA>
This element allows the web author to specify an area of the form that the respondent can use to write text, such as comments, further information and so on. As you'll expect by now, if this area was completed to say, for example "I'm interested in your Chemical database" the returned section of the form would read:

Trial request for: I'm interested in your Chemical database

<INPUT TYPE="SUBMIT" VALUE="Send your
response to us">
<INPUT TYPE="RESET" VALUE="Clear values
and start over">
These are the last two areas of the form, to allow the respondent either to send it to you, or to delete everything that they've already filled in and begin again. The VALUE element here can contain any

text that you wish – the button will automatically re-size itself to fit.

As I mentioned at the very beginning, forms can be used in a variety of ways, and this is just one sample. You can explore forms in more detail by visiting an online form maker at http://www.nytebyte.com/business/cgisamp/formaker.htm which will actually create them for you, and provide you with the HTML code so you can cut and paste it into your own page!

7. Tables

Tables are an extremely useful tool in the web author's armoury. Not only can they be used in the way in which you would expect, but they can also be a very helpful way of positioning data on the screen, giving you control over the appearance of the page. There are a lot of different variables you can include, such as the size of the grid, background colours, spreading a cell across columns or rows and so on.

However, let's begin by creating a simple table for opening hours through the week, so it has 5 columns and 2 rows, as seen in Figure 10.

Opening hours

Monday	Tuesday	Wednesday	Thursday	Friday
9.00 - 17.00	9.00 - 16.00	9.00 - 13.00	13.00 - 17.00	Closed

Figure 10

```
<TABLE BORDER>
<CAPTION>Opening hours</CAPTION>
<TR>
<TH>Monday</TH>
<TH>Tuesday</TH>
<TH>Wednesday</TH>
<TH>Thursday</TH>
<TH>Friday</TH>
</TR>
```

```
<TR>
<TD>9.00 - 17.00</TD>
<TD>9.00 - 16.00</TD>
<TD>9.00 - 13.00</TD>
<TD>13.00 - 17.00</TD>
<TD>Closed</TD>
</TR>
</TABLE>
```

<TABLE BORDER>

The <TABLE> . . . </TABLE> tags create the table for you, and everything that you put into the table must be between these two. The most common attribute for the tag is the BORDER attribute, which causes the table to be drawn with a border around it. You certainly don't need to include it; if you don't have a border to your table one won't appear (obviously!) and this can be useful for laying data out on the page; you'd be amazed at the number of pages which are actually just really big tables!

<CAPTION> . . . </CAPTION>

This is also a tag that isn't required, but can be quite useful if you want to have a nice neat table. You won't run into any problems if you leave it out.

<TR>
<TH>Monday</TH>
</TR>

Each table row is indicated by the <TR> . . . </TR> tag. You can have as many rows as you want, of course, and as many cells as you wish; just remember to make sure that each row has the same number of cells, or your table will display badly, or in some cases, not at all. In the first example, of the days of the week, I used the <TH> . . . </TH> tag to indicate that each cell was also a table heading, so as you can see from Figure 10, the text in each cell is in bold type.

<TR>
<TD>9.00 - 17.00</TD>
</TR>

The tag for creating a table row is <TR> . . .</TR> and within the row, you must then define each cell in turn, together with its contents, which is where the <TD> . . . </TD> comes into play, which of course means Table Data. I've included contents for each cell, but if you want to leave a cell empty, you can add the
 (break) tag. As well as having text in a cell, or leaving the cell blank, you can also include images for example, simply by including the appropriate tag for the image (as discussed in Chapter 5) in place of any text.

Cell alignment

You may find that there are times when you want to align the contents of a cell, and there are HTML tags that will achieve this for you, either on the horizontal or vertical plane. This is simple to do, as you just need to add in the appropriate tag and variable. We've already seen that you can align paragraphs by LEFT CENTER RIGHT and they are matched by TOP CENTER BOTTOM (vertical or v align) so if you wanted to set the default for an entire row, an example of the HTML code that you would use is:

```
<TR ALIGN=CENTER VALIGN=TOP>
```

The same tags can of course be used on individual cells; you just have to use the variables with the <TD> tag instead.

Spanning rows and columns

So far we have just looked at individual cells and empty cells, but there will be times when you want a single cell to span several rows or columns. Let's work a little bit more with our opening hours table to see what else we can add, as seen in Figure 11.

Opening hours

The Library				
Monday	**Tuesday**	**Wednesday**	**Thursday**	**Friday**
9.00 - 17.00	9.00 - 16.00	9.00 - 13.00	13.00 - 17.00	Closed

Figure 11

```
<TR>
<TH COLSPAN=5>The Library</TH>
</TR>
```
I created a new heading (The Library), and the COLSPAN=5 ensured that this new heading spanned all the way across the table. Cells always span downwards and to the right, so you need to add the variable in the correct cell. If I wanted to span downwards, I could have used ROWSPAN to achieve that particular effect.

Table sizes

As you may have noticed from the examples above, the browser itself works out how large to make the table cells, based on the data that is in each of them. While this makes life easier, you may well end up with a table that is not visually appealing. However, there will be times when you want to exert control over this for yourself. You may be able to achieve this with cells that contain text by using the <BR> tag, so it's always worthwhile trying that to begin with. For the times when that doesn't do the job for you, the first thing to consider is changing the size of the entire table, by adding in a WIDTH attribute to the <TABLE> tag. This attribute can be either in terms of pixels, or as a percentage of the current screen width. I generally find it is a better practice to use a percentage, rather than pixels, because I don't know how large the screen is that the viewer is using, and if the width of the table is larger than their screen the table disappears off the right hand side of the screen, and they then have to scroll across in order to view the thing in its entirety.

Opening hours				
The Library				
Monday	Tuesday	Wednesday	Thursday	Friday
9.00 - 17.00	9.00 - 16.00	9.00 - 13.00	13.00 - 17.00	Closed

Figure 12

83

```
<TABLE BORDER WIDTH=75%>
```

As you can see; it's very easy to change the size of the table this way.

Instead of changing the size of the entire table, I might simply want to change the size of individual column widths. The WIDTH attribute can be used in exactly the same with both <TH> <TD> tags.

Other table attributes

We've almost finished with tables now, but there are just a few other small details that we need to cover. Earlier I briefly mentioned the border. You can change the size of the border by adding in a variable from 0-9 (0 means that no border will be added, and 9 means it will be very thick). This only applies to the border around the entire table, not to individual cells, so if you want to have thicker internal borders around cells, you can use the CELLSPACING attribute.

Opening hours

The Library

Monday	Tuesday	Wednesday	Thursday	Friday
9.00 - 17.00	9.00 - 16.00	9.00 - 13.00	13.00 - 17.00	Closed

Fig 13

```
<TABLE BORDER=5 CELLSPACING=3 WIDTH=75%>
```

By now it should be clear as to how the attributes work in practice.

Finally, if you want to change the background colour to a table, in order to make it stand out rather more, you can use the tag BGCOLOR="..." in the <TABLE> tag. If you want to know more about this, it's covered in the very next chapter, where I talk about colour in a little more detail.

8. Colour on your pages

I've talked quite extensively about graphics elsewhere, so don't intend to repeat myself unnecessarily here. However, it is worth briefly saying a few words about background colours and images.

Background images

The default background for a web page is a rather dirty grey. Perfectly acceptable, lots of people use it, but it's rather boring. You may decide that you want to add a little more colour and interest to your pages, and an easy way of doing this is to add a background image to the page. This can be done quite simply by adding a BACKGROUND attribute to the <BODY> element like this:

```
<BODY BACKGROUND="filename.gif">
```

Background graphics are often referred to as 'textures' and there are a great many of these available for use; good graphics packages should include some for you to use. The background image is retrieved by the browser and repeated across and down the page, so it is important that the image you choose lines up correctly on all four sides, or you will end up with a background that looks messy and unprofessional. If you want to create your own I would suggest using a graphics package that has a utility that will do this for you, since it's almost impossible to get background images to line up properly without one.

The other point I'd like to make regarding backgrounds is not to chose a complicated one, or one that will interfere with the text – you do after all want the viewer to be able to read the text on the screen! Once you have found and experimented with your background image don't forget to print out a sample page to make sure that printers can cope with the image. If the particular page in question is one that you want people to be able to print out (such as an article, handout or list of instructions), it may be more sensible to add colour as a background, rather than an image.

Background colours

As stated, the default background for most browsers is a dirty grey (or silver grey if you want to be kind). You can define a coloured background for your page by adding the BGCOLOR (note American spelling again) to your <BODY> element like this:

```
<BODY BGCOLOR="#nnnnnn">
```

where 'nnnnnn' is a triplet of hex numbers representing the RGB (Red, Green and Blue) values (from 0 to 255 or a series of characters) of the colour you want to use. The # (hash sign) must precede the hex triplet otherwise it won't work. Some example colours are:

```
Black     #000000
White     #FFFFFF
Navy      #000080
```

```
Blue            #0000FF
Cyan           #00FFFF
Green           #00FF00
Yellow         #FFFF00
Red            #FF0000
Magenta        #FF00FF
```

Text colours

Default colours for text are of course black for normal text and blue underline for links, with another colour (often purple, but this may vary according to your browser and monitor) for followed links.

There may be times when you want to change the default colours for example to emphasise something in particular. Although you can also change the links and followed links colours it's perhaps best to leave them as they are, since people are used to skimming over a page looking for links, and if you've chosen another colour it may result in confusion.

To change the font colour, all the text must be surrounded by the appropriate tag, so it will look something like this:

```
<FONT COLOR="#FF0000">New this month!</FONT>
```

which will result in the text (New this month!) being displayed in red.

If you really want to go wild with your colours try the following out:

```
<BODY BGCOLOR="#FFFF00" TEXT="#FF0000"
LINK="#400040" VLINK="#C0C0C0">
```

since this will set a background colour, a different colour for all the text, yet another colour for links and a final colour for followed links. It's not a selection I'd choose for my pages, but you might find it fun to try out just once! (All the tags should be obvious, except perhaps the last, which is the one for followed links).

9. Frames

HTML support for frames was introduced several years ago, and for a while there was a fashion for including them on Web pages; almost every page that you visited was a frames-based site. Thankfully however, that fashion does seem to have passed now, and they are not nearly as common as they were. In my opinion, there are very few occasions when frames are appropriate for a site; they can prove to be a useful navigation aid, but other than that I'm doubtful about their use, though I accept that I'm probably slightly biased about this!

Another important point regarding frames is that not all search engines are able to index frames sites, although this number is decreasing all the time. As a result, you may find that you get a worse ranking with some engines than you will with others.

However, all that I'll say is 'think really, really hard about including them'. If you've decided that you do want frames on your pages, I'll explain exactly how you go about it. Let's start by looking at how they work, then move onto the appropriate HTML tags to create them.

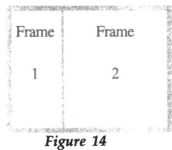

Figure 14

Figure 14 shows an imaginary page. For the sake of argument, Frame 1 will contain a menu, and when any option is clicked, the appropriate page will load into Frame 2. The contents of each frame will be a different HTML file. In order to create a web page that displays the frames correctly it is necessary to create a frame definition document, which contains the layout and names of the HTML documents that are to be included. To create the above example, the coding would look like this:

```
<HTML>
<HEAD>
<TITLE>Blank</TITLE>
</HEAD>

<FRAMESET COLS="18%,82%">
<FRAME SRC="menu.htm" NAME="menu">
<FRAME SRC="intro.htm" NAME="main"
MARGINWIDTH="3" MARGINHEIGHT="3"
SCROLLING="YES">

<NOFRAMES>
<BODY>
</BODY>
</NOFRAMES>
</FRAMESET>
</HTML>
```

<FRAMESET COLS="18%,82%">
This tag tells the browser how to set up the page, and in this example I want columns, one being 18% of the screen, the other 82% of the screen. Of course, if you wanted the screen split horizontally instead of vertically, you should use ROWS instead, in exactly the same way.

<FRAME SRC="menu.htm" NAME="menu">
Next, you need to tell the browser what each frame is called, and which files you want displayed where. So, in this example, I've called the left hand frame 'menu' and, to make my life a little easier, I'll also create an HTML file with the same name.

<FRAME SRC="intro.htm" NAME="main"
MARGINWIDTH="3"
MARGINHEIGHT="3"SCROLLING="YES">
I've also had to do the same for the larger window (called NAME="main") and decide on the file that will be automatically loaded into the frame when someone visits the site. The second and third attributes set the size of the margins, while the last allows the user to scroll down the frame.

<NOFRAMES><BODY></BODY></
NOFRAMES>
It's an unfortunate fact of life that not everyone uses more recent versions of browsers, and some very old ones will not support the use of frames. As a result, you need to be able to provide them with some information, or all that will be seen is a blank screen, which really isn't a good idea, for obvious reasons. If you include text as normal within the <BODY> . . . </BODY> tags as usual, such disadvantaged users will be able to see something, even if it's only 'I'm sorry, but this site uses frames. Please update your browser'!

Now, if we just stopped at this point, we'd have our frames page, and two HTML files being loaded. However, this isn't going to be enough, since if we're using a menu in Frame 1 and we click on an option, it will automatically load into Frame 1, instead of Frame 2. Consequently, we need to be able to inform the browser in some way that when a menu item is chosen, it loads into Frame 2 (which you'll remember I called 'main').

<A HREF="events.htm" TARGET="main">Library Events</A>

To do this, we must make use of the <A> . . . </A> tag once again, since we're creating a link from one document to another. So, in our menu.htm page if we include a link such as the one above, the browser knows that when this link is followed, it should load the file called 'events.htm' into the target window that I called 'main'.

As you might expect, things can get very much more complicated very quickly, but the above should be enough to allow you to start creating your own frames pages, if you must!

10. JavaScript and CGI

JavaScript

I'll start this section with an apology; it's not possible to properly cover the use of JavaScript in the space that I have available; books the size of doorstops are written on the subject, so even if I dedicated this entire book to JavaScript I couldn't adequately cover the subject. Consequently, I'll simply try to give an outline of what JavaScript is, and how it is used, together with some suggested resources so that you can follow them up for yourself if you find that this is an area that you'd like to explore in more detail.

JavaScript is a programming language that used to be called 'LiveScript', and it was written to improve HTML functionality and to add more features to Web pages. It should not be confused with Sun Microsystems Java programming language, which is a fully-fledged language in its own right.

JavaScript is integrated directly into an HTML document, rather than being stored as a separate file, and as a result is run directly by the browser, and most recent versions of browsers are compatible with JavaScript, although more elderly versions will not be able to run the scripts. You may also find that some companies and organisations will not allow their staff to access pages that contain JavaScript because of the potential danger to their network security. (It is possible to create a script that would interrogate your hard drive for example, and pass the information it finds onto a third party, although I have to say that I think this is a remote possibility at best).

As a result, you can use a variety of applets to create interesting effects on web pages, as well as rather more complicated applications. In order to explain how JavaScript works, let's take a look at a simple example, which is used to create a mouse rollover effect on a web page. Again, given the limitations of hard copy I can't actually show it in action, but I hope the following figures 15 and 16 give you a good idea.

Figure 15   *Figure 16*

Fig 15 shows a real life example from my own website (http://www.philb.com) with a menu/navigation bar on the left hand side of the screen. When the cursor is moved over any of the options the black text changes into red, and the little folder icon opens, as seen in Fig 16

```
<SCRIPT LANGUAGE="Javascript">

<!--
browserVer = parseInt(navigator.appVersion);
browserName = navigator.appName;
if (browserVer >= 4) {
    version = "v4";
}
else {
    if (browserName == "Netscape" &&
    browserVer >=3) {
        version = "v4";
    }
    else {
      version = "v3";
    }
}

if (version == "v4") {
btn1up = new Image();
btn4up.src = "article.gif";
btn4dn = new Image();
btn4dn.src = "article1.gif";

}

function btnUp(imgName) {
    if (version == "v4") {
      imgOn = eval(imgName + "up.src");
      document.images[imgName].src = imgOn;

  }
}

function btnDn(imgName) {
    if (version == "v4") {
       imgOff = eval(imgName + "dn.src")
       document.images[imgName].src = imgOff;
  }
}
//-->

</SCRIPT>
```

*<SCRIPT LANGUAGE="Javascript"> . . . </
SCRIPT>*
This tag tells the browser that anything within the
tags is to be treated as a script, and that it should
execute the appropriate commands contained
within it. The tag should be placed inside the
<HEAD> . . . </HEAD> tag, rather than anywhere
else.

<!-- //-->
As some old or unsophisticated browsers don't
understand JavaScript it is also necessary to sur-
round the script with a tag that the browser will
take to mean a comment, and it will be ignored. As
a result, these browsers will still show the page,
even if they are unable to display it in quite the
way that the author would like.

I'm not going to go through all of the tags in turn
as I've done with the other examples that I've used,
simply because of space considerations. However
if you take a look through the script you'll see that
there is a reference to an image entitled article.gif
and that section of the JavaScript tells the browser
that if the cursor is moved over that particular image it should load a second image to replace the
first, resulting in the rather attractive mouse rollover
effect. (In case you're wondering, I deleted the extra code for all the other images to save space).

If you're interested in finding out more about
JavaScript, I'd suggest that you take a look at: http:/
/ w e b r e f e r e n c e . c o m / p r o g r a m m i n g /
javascript.html

CGI Scripting

CGI stands for Common Gateway Interface, which is a way of running programs on the server, based on the input from the user at the Web page, such as to add comments to a Web-based bulletin board for example. CGI scripts therefore differ from JavaScript in that the programming is done behind the scenes, rather than by utilising the browser to achieve the result. If you've ever used a web page search engine, it's very likely that you've made use of a CGI script, even though you didn't realise it at the time.

How CGI scripts work

You visit a page, and are invited to fill out a comments form for inclusion on a guest book for example. Once you've filled out the form and clicked on 'send' or 'add' or whatever the author has called the submission button, the data is passed onto a CGI script which is running on the remote server. The script then performs whatever actions are required, in this case adding your comments to another webpage, and perhaps taking you to the guest book page, or taking you to a 'thank you' page instead.

Let's take another example, and look at the CGI script. Imagine a web page that has a link to 'Show me today's date', and when you click on that, you get shown the date. The CGI script might look a little like this:

```
<A HREF="http://www.mysite.co.uk/cgi-bin/
getdate">Show me today's date</A>
```

The <A> ... </A> tag points the browser to a sub-directory and script called cgi-bin/getdate and the script is written in such a way as to display the date on a new page. Therefore as you can see, all the browser does is to find the script, based on the location the author has provided, lets the script run, then does as it is told.

You may or may not be able to use CGI scripts yourself; this depends on the way in which your remote server has been set up. (We'll talk more about this later in Chapter 12). If you pay for space you'll almost certainly have a cgi-bin sub-directory, but if your web space comes free as part of the package offered by your Internet Service Provider (ISP) you may find that you cannot run scripts at all, or only a small selection as provided by the ISP.

Once again, I'm afraid that there isn't space available in this book to go into the details of exactly what scripts are available, and how to write them. However, there are a great many CGI libraries available on the Web, and I would encourage you to go and explore them, such as http://www.htmlgoodies.com. Most of these libraries offer scripts entirely free of charge and which have already been written for you, so it is only necessary to change a small number of variables (such as the URL of your site) within them in order to make them work. However, before you find one and start to alter it to work on your site, please do check with your ISP to see if you can use it! If you can't, all is not lost, since there are web sites that will run scripts for you, and all you need to do is to add the appropriate anchor to their site and scripts.

Some of these are commercial services, while others are free, but you have to put up with advertising banners at the top of your new guest book for example.

11. Meta tags

I briefly mentioned meta tags earlier – they are used by some search engines to assist in ranking your pages. I cannot overestimate the use of them; you should have meta tags on each and every page that you produce. This chapter explains in more detail how they work, and provides examples of them in use.

If you simply produce your home page and register the URL with a search engine, or a number of search engines, their spider programmes will (eventually) visit your site to index it. Now, each of the search engines does· this slightly differently. AltaVista for example will grab everything in your document and index it, but will only show the first 250 characters in its description. Consequently, if your site included, say, 'Thanks to:....' right at the beginning, this is what AltaVista would show in its description, and it wouldn't give the viewer any idea of what your site actually covered. Of course, not all search engines work this way; I'd suggest you ferret around a little bit to see exactly how the popular engines work, and certainly the major ones such as AltaVista, Lycos, Yahoo, Infoseek and Excite. It therefore makes sense to ensure that your opening paragraph is carefully written so that it accurately reflects what your site covers.

However, you may be able to exert a certain amount of control over how your site is indexed by the use of the meta tag. (I should however point out that not all search engines will use this tag – AltaVista does, but at the time of writing Excite doesn't, for example.) It's not a total cure-all therefore, but you won't miss out by putting the tag in, and it may work well in some cases.

What does a meta tag look like?

You should insert the meta tag element at the top of your document, just after the <TITLE> element. It follows the usual form of tags, i.e.

```
<META name="something" content="something
else">
```

but note that you don't have to have a </META> at the end of the tag, the way that you do with something like <BOLD> . . . </BOLD>. However, make sure that each tag does not include any line breaks, since some search engines get a little bit upset about this.

What can I include in a meta tag?

There are basically four major meta tags that you can use:

*<META name="resource-type"
content="document">*
The only resource type that is currently in use is "document" This is the only tag that you need to put in for indexing purposes, but use of the others is a good idea.

<META name="description" content="a description of your page">
Depending on the search engine, this will be displayed along with the title of your page in an index; "content" could be a word, sentence or even paragraph to describe your page. Keep this reasonably short, concise and to the point. However, don't be so mean with your description that it's not an appropriate reflection of the contents!

<META name="keywords" content="a, list, of, keywords, and some phrases, or, words">
Choose whatever keywords you think are appropriate, separated by commas. Remember to include synonyms, americanisms and so on. So, if you had a page on cars, you might want to include keywords such as car, cars, vehicles, automobiles and so on. If you wish to include a phrase, just place a comma at the very end of the phrase.

<META name="distribution" content="one of several">
Content should contain either global, local or iu (for Internal Use). To be perfectly honest, I can't quite get my head around this one; it's supposed to list available resources designed to allow the user to find things easily, but I still don't quite get it. My advice is to stick to "global".

Other optional tags

There are a lot of other tags, and I've included a few examples below. Only add them if you really think there is a use for them, otherwise exclude them; it won't hurt at all.

<META name="copyright" content="copyright statement">
Pretty obvious what this one's for.

<META HTTP-EQUIV="varname" content="data">
This binds the varname to an HTTP header field. An http server might use this to process a document. This one's a little more tricky. If you included the following example:

<META HTTP-EQUIV="keywords" content="car,cars">
then, as part of a GET command the server would include the word car and cars in the HTTP response header. (If this doesn't make sense, don't worry about it, I'm only including it for the sake of completion).

<META HTTP-EQUIV="refresh" content="0; url=homepage.htm">
This can be used in the <HEAD> section of any .htm(l) file to redirect it to homepage.htm. The figure after content is the time in seconds that the browser waits before moving on. This can be quite a useful one if you want to automatically move someone from one page to another.

There are a few others that you can include, such as "revisit-after" and "rating" if you want to be really comprehensive.

12. Publishing your pages

I hope that by now you have had an opportunity to create some web pages locally, and run them on the browser on your computer. I suspect that by now you're keen to get your site up and running on the Internet so that everyone else can see what you've achieved. Therefore, in this chapter I'll cover exactly how you go about doing just that.

The first thing that you must do is to decide on the name of your site, or your domain name. Mine is www.philb.com for example. Yours may have already been established; almost certainly if you're from an academic institution or a large commercial organisation. Alternatively, you may decide to use any free web space that you have been allocated by your ISP. In these cases the URL will have been decided upon, and short of going out and getting a new URL you're stuck with what you've got, good or bad. If that's the case with you, feel free to skip the next couple of paragraphs.

What makes a good domain name?

Unless you live your life as a hermit you'll see domain names all around you; on the way to visit a client recently I counted over 30 different domain names that I noticed in newspapers, on advertising hoardings, on the sides of taxis and on flyers that were handed out to me. A good domain name should be memorable, and hopefully should be linked to you or your company in some way. If people can remember it they are more likely to tell their friends and colleagues, include it in any written communications and so on. You will also find that an increasing number of search engines allow people to do a search for the URL, and will give a high level of relevance to those pages that include any search terms, so it's very important to get the name correct right at the beginning.

The first thing to do is to think of a few possible choices for your name. If it's a personal site, perhaps your fore-name, or surname, for example. (Although I should warn you at the outset that most of these have already been taken by other individuals – I tried to get www.phil.com but unfortunately that had already been taken). When you've thought of a few alternatives you will need to check and see if they are available, and you can do this quite simply by doing what is known as a DNS search (Domain Name System), using one of the many search engines on the Internet that are designed for this process. You might want to use http:// www.totalweb.co.uk/tws-bin/checkdomain.cgi if you want to get started quickly.

Should I chose .com, .co.uk, .org or .org.uk?

Obviously if you're part of the academic, government or military community you will be able to use .ac, .gov or .mil as appropriate, and as I mentioned above, this will in all probability have already been set up for you. However, if you are working for a commercial or charitable organisation you might have to make the choice yourself. In the 'old days' (by which I mean the past three or four years) .com was used by American commercial organisations, .co.uk by British commercial companies, .org or .org.uk by non-profit making organisations in the US or UK respectively. However, more recently this system has fallen into disuse, and many people (such as myself) will opt for a .com address. There are good reasons for doing this. Many browsers will default to .com in the location/address box, so if you just type 'philb' to reach my site, both Netscape and Explorer will automatically add .com to the end of it and will connect to my site. If I had gone for a .co.uk site I might be missing out on getting people to come to my site. Secondly, people are increasingly viewing .com addresses as 'serious', which I personally think is rather stupid, but it is so. My advice here is that if you are promoting your site to a global audience, try and get a .com address, but if you are only interested in visitors say from the UK, or the content is specifically tailored to a UK based audience, go for a .co.uk address instead. The same can be said if you're a non-profit-making organisation – go for .org or .org.uk as appropriate.

So, having decided on your domain name, the next step is to register it, and obtain some web space to go with it. In most cases, companies that offer web space will also register the domain name for you, saving you a little time and trouble. If you want to learn more about the process before you register (and also to check current costs and any legal issues) you may wish to visit http:// www.nominet.net/ which is the national registry for all Internet Domain Names ending in .uk but even if you want a .com domain name, it's still worth spending some time at this site, which provides valuable and authoritative information.

Choosing a web hosting service

There are literally hundreds of companies now offering this particular service. You can pay anything from nothing at all (by going through one of the free ISP's, though as already mentioned, you'll have to accept that the URL is given to you, rather than you choosing the one you want), to companies that want many hundreds of pounds per year. All of the Internet magazines will have advertising supplements, and it is worth browsing through those to see who offers the best deals. All good web hosting companies will have a list of clients, and it is worth emailing a few of them to ask what sort of service they've been given in the past.

Check to see how much space you get, though unless you want a really large site, or have a lot of photographs to put up you won't be able to use as much as you're given. You should also get a cgi-bin directory, as discussed above, and some scripts to go with it. Some companies will also offer audio and/or video streaming facilities as well.

Preparing your site for publication

The easiest way to prepare your site is to create a mirror version of it on your own hard disk or network. Set up the sub-directory structures that you need, and make sure that all your files are in the right place. This is also a good time to tidy up things. You may find that all your files are in a root directory, or jumbled together in a single sub-directory. While this isn't so much of a problem on the local site, you will find that things get messy very quickly. Once you've moved your pages around and put them in the correct place, test your pages again. This is particularly important if you have linked graphics into the same directory as the pages you've written. (You'll remember that in Chapter 3 I said that I'd come back to this point). If you create a sub-directory called 'images' or 'graphics' and put your images into that, you'll need to point the browser to the correct sub-directory so that it can find and display them properly. Consequently, your tags will need to reflect this. If your tag looked like this for example

```
<IMG SRC="kilroy.gif" ALT="Horizontal Line"
WIDTH="560" HEIGHT="26">
```

and you've moved the .GIF into a graphics directory you'll need to change the tag to look like:

```
<IMG SRC="/graphics/kilroy.gif"
ALT="Horizontal Line" WIDTH="560"
HEIGHT="26">
```

so that the browser can then find the graphics sub-directory and display the image correctly. This is known as a 'relative' URL, since the position of the graphics sub-directory is relative to the position of the HTML file that is being read by the browser. An 'absolute' URL would be something like: <IMG SRC="http://www.mysite.co.uk/graphics/kilroy.gif" . . . >

Relative or absolute URL's?

How you reference your pages and images is of course entirely up to you. However, I tend to prefer to write relative URL's, because that's the way that I work with my clients. For example, if I'm producing test pages for a client to look at, the directory structure on my site would look like this:

/html/clients/xyzclient/index.html

If I produced web pages with absolute URL's they would have to be addressed to this particular location, and once I moved the pages to the client's own site, the addresses would need to be changed for all of the links. By writing relative links I can move the entire sub-directory to its new location without having to change anything.

Naming your files

You should give each file you create a sensible name, and there are several good reasons for this. It will make it easier for you to find the right file in the future, and more importantly, if you're on leave or move to a new position it will make it easier for someone to take over the management of your web site. Furthermore, as previously mentioned, sophisticated search engines can run searches on URL's, so if someone is looking for pages about the library for example, your page will stand a better chance of getting a good ranking (or indeed, being found at all!) if the URL is along the lines of http://www.mysite.co.uk/library.htm or even better, http://www.mysite.co.uk/library/library_hours.htm

You are at liberty to chose to end your file names with .htm or .html as both are acceptable to browsers. In the early days of web creation, they were mainly written in and for a UNIX system, which works with long extensions, so it made sense to call the extension .html for HyperText Markup Language. However, when people began writing pages under a Windows system, which only allowed a three letter extension this became shortened to .htm. Chose whichever you prefer, but do ensure that you are consistent in your choice, otherwise you will find it difficult to remember which extension a particular file has and increase the chances of getting the anchor incorrect, causing the link to fail.

The only file name that is really important is that for your home, or introductory page, which should always be called 'index.htm(l)' (you still have the choice of adding the extra 'l' however). This is the default file that the browser will look for, allowing you to publish a shorter address in written communication, http://www.philb.com and http://www.philb.com/index.htm both point to exactly the same file.

Once you've prepared everything, take a few moments to double check. Are all your files named sensibly? Do they all end in either .htm or .html? Are all the files and associated directories in lower case, or if you've chosen a mixture of upper and lower case names, do the links point correctly? Have you named your graphics files correctly?

When satisfied, you can go onto the next stage.

Uploading the pages to your webspace

In order to do this, you need to have a special program that will connect to your webspace, and allow you to copy the files across from the hard disk on your computer. The generic name for this utility is an FTP package, or File Transfer Protocol package. There are a great many of these, some free, some commercial. You can obtain a list of them from http://dir.yahoo.com/Business_and_Economy/ Companies/Computers/Business_to_Business/ Software/Internet/FTP/

Your FTP package works very much like the Windows Explorer utility, in that it allows you to create directories, move files, delete or rename them at will. More sophisticated packages will have extra facilities, but unless you're going to be doing a lot of FTP work this won't be necessary. The package that I use is one called WS_FTP and you can see what it looks like in operation in figure 17.

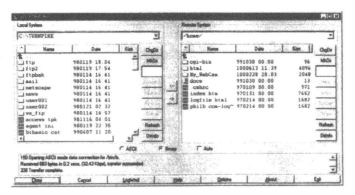

Figure 17

The left-hand side of the screen shows my local hard drive directory structure, and the right-hand side of the screen shows the remote system that holds the directory structure and files that are available on the Web. In order to copy a file from the local machine to the remote server it is simply a question of clicking the correct file and dragging it into the appropriate sub-directory. If you can use Windows Explorer, you can use an FTP package; it's no more complicated. There is really only one thing that you need to take care of, which is the way in which the file is copied; either as ASCII or Binary. Images should always be copied as binaries, while text files (all your .htm(l) files) can be copied as either. You'll see the appropriate options just beneath the two windows in Figure 17.

Testing your pages

Once you have uploaded all your files the next thing to do is to check them to make sure that they work. If possible, do this on another machine, rather than the one that you used to create your pages. The reason for doing this is as follows:

If you've made a mistake with one of your anchors, it is possible that it will address an image, for example, that is on your own machine. The tag might look like this:

```
<IMG SRC="///C|/Phil/graphics/kilroy.gif"
ALT="Horizontal Line" WIDTH="560"
HEIGHT="26">
```

which tells the browser to look on the C: drive in a directory called Phil and a sub-directory called graphics. (This will generally only happen if you use an authoring tool, but I'll talk more about this later).

If you published the page with an anchor like that, and someone else pointed their browser at the page, it would be instructed to look on the local drive, to find a directory called Phil, check in a sub-directory called graphics and find a file called kilroy.gif, which in all probability wouldn't exist, creating an error. Now, if you go and look at that page on the web, your browser will do exactly the same thing, only this time it will find the file and can display it correctly. You'll simply see the image in place and think that all is well, when in actual fact this is very far from the case. So, if at all possible, view the page(s) on another machine. Of course, this shouldn't happen if you've properly checked all your pages, but we all make mistakes now and then.

When testing, try as many different browsers and versions of browsers that you can, to make sure that you're happy with the final effect you get. If you want to make changes, this is the time to do it, before anyone else gets a chance to see what you've done, and more importantly, what mistakes you've made.

Don't get discouraged if the page doesn't look the way that it should; this is to be expected. Simply go back to the source code, identify where you've gone wrong and correct the mistake. Sometimes it can be very minor; a missing full stop or tag with a missing > for example can cause havoc on a page. If you're unable to find the error you might want to check with one of the online HTML checkers that exist. These are very useful things indeed, and the one that I make use of is called the Web Site Garage at http://www.websitegarage.com which will check your HTML coding, tell you how fast your page loads under optimal conditions, checks the spelling (although as it follows a US English system it's not that helpful!), checks your meta tags and so on.

Registering your site with search engines

Once you're happy with your site, all the links work, and all the graphics load correctly, it's time to tell the world about it. The easiest way of doing this is to register the site with as many different search engines as you think are appropriate. There are basically two ways of doing this; you can do it manually yourself, or you can use a submission agent to do it on your behalf.

Registering manually

This is very straightforward and easy, but it is time consuming. Before you start, have a list of your keywords and page descriptions handy, because you may need them. Visit the search engine(s) that you want to register your pages with, and look for a link on the page which says something like 'Add URL' or 'Register your site' or something similar. Click on the link and follow the instructions. They will all ask for the URL of your site, so start by just giving the URL for your home or index page. Some of them may ask for more information, which is where the keywords and description come in handy; cut and paste when possible to save time. You should then get a message saying that the page has been visited, indexed or spidered, and the page should be included in the search engine's index in a few hours or days; this isn't a precise science, so be patient.

If you are registering with an Index or Directory based search engine the process is a little more complicated, because you have to hunt through their hierarchy until you find the right section and subsection for your page. At that point look for the 'Add URL' button, and follow the instructions outlined above.

Wait for a few days, then visit the search engine and run a search that should hopefully pull up your own site. To make certain the site is listed you may be able to do a search on the domain name; some search engines allow you to search using syntax such as host:www.mysite.co.uk and it will return a list of results of the pages that it knows of on your site.

Automatic registration

If all of this seems like too much work, you can employ a submission agent utility to do the job on your behalf. You simply supply the agent with the details already mentioned, click on the engines you want to register with and let it get on with the job. However, you still have to nursemaid the system, because there will be index/directory search engines and you will need to decide under which category you want to be included. I've used both methods to register pages that I've written and published and although automatic registration saves some time, it's only minutes, rather than hours.

The main disadvantage of using submission agents is that some search engines might not accept a registration provided by an agent, so it's doubly necessary to check after a few days just to make sure that your site has been included.

To register or not to register

You don't have to register your pages at all, it just makes sense. If you don't register your pages search engines will eventually find you, since they spider the Web by going from link to link to link, and once they find a new or revised page, they'll copy the data back home and include the newly found pages at that point. However, it may take several months before this happens, so for that period of time the only people that will know about your site are the ones that you've told yourself.

The other point worth bringing out here, which I've just implied, is that you don't need to register every page individually. Just register your index.htm(l) page, and the search engine(s) will follow links to all your other pages and index them automatically. You will only need to register pages individually if you've added a new one, or updated an older one and it's important to you that everyone knows about this.

You should also put aside some time every couple of months to go back and re-register your pages.

Some search engines have the distressing habit of losing pages that were in their index, so it's worthwhile reminding them every now and then.

Checking your positioning

Once you have submitted your site to the various search engines, wait for a few days, then check to see how well you have done, by searching for your keywords to see if your site comes up in the first few hits returned by the engines you use. A good way of doing this is to use a utility such as Rank This! at http://www.rankthis.com/ which will tell you where your site comes when using a particular keyword. (More details can be obtained from the site itself or from the Know How guide *How to promote your web site effectively*, by Mark Kerr.)

13. Authoring tools

If you have been following the examples in this book and trying out a few of your own you are probably getting tired of using a text editor such as Notepad. It's slow, laborious, and it's easy to make mistakes – even missing a single character, or putting it in the wrong place can result in a page that doesn't load correctly or even at all.

Luckily however, a great many software packages exist to make life easier when it comes to writing web pages, and these are generally referred to as 'authoring tools' for fairly obvious reasons. In many respects their interfaces look like those you'd expect to find with word processors; small icons to embolden, italicise, to add in graphics, and so on. More expensive packages will also include graphics utilities, animation software, templates, JavaScript applets, cgi scripts and so on. They will also allow you to import files from other packages such as word processors and will automatically work with them to add in appropriate tags, therefore greatly reducing the work that you have to do. Cheaper or free packages won't in general have as many extras, but will nonetheless produce good code for you.

There is no one 'best' package; it depends entirely on what you want to do, and how complex your site is, so you might find it's worthwhile trying out a few packages to see which one you feel most comfortable with. You can either download them from the company's website or copy them from the cover discs of the many Internet magazines. Alternatively, visit:

```
h t t p : / / d i r . y a h o o . c o m /
Computers_and_Internet/Software/Reviews/
Titles/Internet/Web_Authoring_Tools/
HTML_Editors/
```

which will provide you with links to many of them.

It will obviously take you some time to get used to the authoring tool you use, just as with any other complex program, and because there are so many of them, I can't give you much in-depth detail, because it will differ from program to program. However, most packages will give you the option of displaying your content in three different ways – with HTML tags on, with them turned off, or in a WYSIWYG (What You See Is What You Get) format. Most allow you simply to highlight a word and choose the appropriate icon to click on to embolden, italicise and so on. Importing data is also a key feature, and the more sophisticated the package, the larger the number of formats you can import from (such as word processing packages, databases and so on), and they will automatically insert the correct HTML code for you.

Most will also allow you to publish your Web pages as well, and this is an area that you need to be aware of. When you initially write your pages, and choose to include a graphic for example, the package will allow you to browse your hard disk to find the image and will then insert it into the page, but it will have local links to the directory and sub-directory on your hard disk. When you then put the pages live, these links have to be changed to reflect the fact that they now sit on the remote server, rather than on your hard disk. If you forget to make these changes your pages will not work correctly. Therefore, immediately prior to putting your pages on the Web, you should make sure that the local links are replaced with remote links, pointing to the server.

14. Adding multimedia to a page

Having put in your text and some graphics you may still want to give your pages a little something extra, or you may have some material that you want to publish that is not suited to either text or static images. Consequently, you may want to consider adding sound or moving images to your pages.

There are advantages and disadvantages to doing this, as you'd expect. Your pages will certainly be more interesting and may well also be more informative, but may take longer to load, and if you add sound to your page in such a way that viewers have no control over it you run the risk that they will simply leave, and leave quickly, never to return!

Adding sound

There are a number of different file formats that you can use to add sound to your pages, but the two major formats are those which end in .wav or .mid. The former are often produced by recording the sound in a digital form and second by second are quite large. The latter are produced using a sound card or MIDI (Musical Instrument Digital Interface) instrument and are rather more effective in terms of file size.

There are several different ways in which you can make a sound play on a web page, and perhaps the easiest is to use the <EMBED> tag. If you imagine that you have a sound file called hallo.mid and you want this to play on your page the HTML code looks like this:

```
<EMBED src="hallo.mid" autostart="true"
loop="true" hidden="true">
```

autostart="true"
This tag ensures that the sound file begins to play as soon as the browser has downloaded it to the local hard disk.

loop="true"
This makes the browser repeat the sound file over and over, rather than just playing it only once.

hidden="true"
This final value means that no control panel is displayed on the page, so the viewer has no control over the sound file being played.

Therefore, this isn't exactly a friendly thing to do, since the sound file starts playing, continues to play and can't be stopped by the viewer – all they can do is turn their sound down or off, or more likely, leave the page. To make things slightly more friendly we could delete the loop="true" variation, which would ensure the sound file played only once. Of course, we could really take pity on the viewer and by deleting the hidden="true" and changing the autostart="true" to "false" it would allow them to decide for themselves if they wanted to listen to the sound file or not. Indeed, by including another tag CONTROLS="smallconsole" the user will then be able to use a little control panel to play, pause, stop or repeat the sound file as they wish. The actual appearance of the control panel will differ according to the browser being used, and the media player installed on the user's system.

A second method, although in my opinion not as good is to use the <BGSOUND> or Background sound tag. It's really only useful if you want to include a background or opening sound, and the tag is not widely supported by all browsers. However, if you want to explore its use, the tag looks like this in operation:

```
<BGSOUND SRC="hallo.mid">
```

and you can include the variables mentioned above to get it to loop over and over again for example.

Other ways of providing sound

Unless you use a small sound file, some users will have problems hearing it, since the larger the file, the longer it will take to download, so they will have visited your site, obtained the information they desired and will have left, all before the file has downloaded sound for them to listen to!

Another option that may be worth considering is audio streaming, which is a better way of providing access to large files, as the user doesn't need to wait for the whole file to download before listening to it. Streaming is commonly used both for large files, and also for live broadcasting and radio web sites.

As you may imagine, audio streaming is rather more complicated, and requires both a server that can cope with this method of provision, and software that will project the sound for you. Consequently, there is little space available in this title to go into this in any detail, but if you wish to explore this in further detail you might like to look at the use of a software package such as Shockwave, which is a product that has been developed by Macromedia at http://www.macromedia.com./shockwave/config.html

Adding video to a page

Once again, there is a variety of different formats that you can use in order to display video on your web page or site. Two common formats are AVI and QuickTime. AVI (audio/video interleaved) is widely used by Video for Windows, the playback is reasonably smooth, interleaving the audio data with each video frame.

QuickTime has been around for a long time, since 1991 in fact, and is the *de facto* standard for desktop video production. QuickTime handles the data rather differently to AVI, since it interleaves in larger blocks, so may appear jerky on a slow modem.

Both formats are cross-platform compatible, though they do both require special programs on the viewer's machine for it to work properly; this is less of a problem with AVI and more so with QuickTime, although since both are widely supported, you have a reasonable chance that your user will have the necessary programs on their machines, but of course you cannot guarentee this!

Whichever route you decide to take, as with images, you will need to get the file size of your video clip as small as you possibly can, so compress it as much as you can. There is a variety of tools available which can help with this, and you might want to visit http://www.tucows.com to chose one.

Putting the video clips on the page is not difficult, and by now you can probably guess how this can be done, either by using the ANCHOR or the EMBED tags, which we've previously looked at. However, just to make the point, you can have a link to a video clip by putting in a link such as:

```
<A HREF="/video/hallo.avi">Hallo!</A>
```

This will result in the user saving the file to their desktop, launching it, or loading a new page to view the clip, depending on the browser and preferences that they have set up.

The second option will of course ensure that the video clip plays as soon as possible, by appearing as the page is being downloaded. However, to ensure that this works correctly the user must have the helper application installed on their machines, so you might want to have a link to the appropriate application. The HTML code is very similar to the audio code that we've just looked at, and uses many of the same variables, so I think that I can just show you an example of the code and let you work it out for yourself!

```
<EMBED SRC="/video/hallo.avi" HEIGHT=200
WIDTH=200 CONTROLLER=TRUE AUTOPLAY=TRUE
LOOP=2>
```

A final word of warning here; downloading images takes more time than downloading text, and the same is even more true of sound and moving images. Always try and give the user the option of choosing to view or listen to the information, rather than forcing it upon them, and remember to provide the information in a text format whenever possible.

15. Further resources

There is probably more information on the Internet about creating Web pages than on any other topic, so any list of resources will only ever be a small selection. I've therefore chosen resources that I have personally found to be of use to me in my work as a web author. Some resources have already been mentioned in the main body of this book, but these are some extra ones that are worthwhile taking a look at.

Creating entire web pages

If you want assistance in creating a page from scratch there are a number of websites that will do exactly that for you. You simply need to fill in the appropriate boxes and the HTML will be created for you. All you then need to do is to cut and paste it into a new document and you will have an instant web page. This can be very useful when starting out in this field as it gives you an opportunity to try out different ideas and see how they are translated into HTML code for you. The following are just a few sample sites that offer this service, for free.

Zyris.com
http://www.zyris.com/

Hayi Homepage Generator
http://www.lafayette.edu/acs/hayi/html-form.html

The "Make Your Own Home Page"
http://www.goliath.org/makepage/
index.html

Creating tables

The TableMaker
http://www.bagism.com/tablemaker/

Colour on your pages

The Colourmaker
http://www.bagism.com/colormaker/

A colour selector for backgrounds, links, text
and so on:
http://www.imagitek.com/bcs.html

Issues on colourblindness:
http://www.cimmerii.demon.co.uk/
colourblind/

Creating frames pages

Framemaker
http://www.bagism.com/frameshop/

Graphics libraries

http://dir.yahoo.com/Arts/Design_Arts/
Graphic_Design/
Web_Page_Design_and_Layout/Graphics/

A1 Graphics
http://www.free-graphics.com/

The Button Hole
http://www.dsuper.net/~zaz/button/
button.html

Designed to a T – free images
http://www.designedtoat.com/index.htm

Web2c backgrounds
http://web2c.com/

Adding sound

http://www.babylon-6.demon.co.uk/
splashra.htm

JavaScript and CGI scripts

http://webreference.com/programming/
javascript.html

Lists of CGI and JavaScripts

http://www.htmlgoodies.com

CGI-Free scripts for anyone to use

http://www.cgi-free.com/

Huge list of CGI scripts

http://www.singlesheaven.com/stas/
TULARC/webmaster/cgi-scripts1.html

FTP Packages

http://dir.yahoo.com/
Business_and_Economy/Companies/Comput-
ers/Business_to_Business/Software/Internet/
FTP/

Cute FTP
http://www.cuteftp.com/

File Dog
http://www.edgepub.com/fd/

WS_FTP Pro
http://www.ipswitch.com/Products/
WS_FTP/index.html

Registering with Search Engines

Submit-it!
http://www.submit-it.com/

The Vault
http://www.the-vault.com/easy-submit/

URL Registration ShareService
http://selfpromotion.com/index.t

Checking page positioning with search engines

Rank This
http://www.rankthis.com

Search Engine Watch
http://www.searchenginewatch.com/

Rating your pages

Recreational Software Advisory Council
http://www.rsac.org/homepage.asp

Legal issues

Internet and electronic rights issues
http://home.earthlink.net/~ivanlove/
internet.html

10 big myths about copyright explained
http://www.clari.net/brad/copymyths.html

Intellectual property online
http://www.eff.org/pub/
Intellectual_property/

The copyright website
http://www.benedict.com/

Page checkers

Dr. Watson
http://watson.addy.com/

Doctor HTML
http://www2.imagiware.com/RxHTML/

Bobby – web pages for people with disabilities
http://www.cast.org/bobby/

The Website Garage
http://websitegarage.netscape.com/

The link checker
http://www.alterego.fr/dev/chkweb.htm

Publicising your site

Goldray
http://goldray.com/register.htm

How to publicize your Web site over the Internet
http://www.samizdat.com/public.html

Promotion World – hints and tips
http://www.promotionworld.com/

Search engine tutorial for promoting web sites
http://northernwebs.com/set/

Virtual Promote
http://192.41.61.81/

Website promotion with WWWPromote
http://wwwpromote.hypermart.net/

Web Promote
http://www.webpromote.com/

General information on HTML and Web page design

W3C home page
http://www.w3.org/MarkUp/

HTML resources on the web
http://www.library.wisc.edu/libraries/Memorial/htmlhelp.htm

The barebones guide to HTML
http://werbach.com/barebones/barebone.html

The HTML Compendium
http://www.htmlcompendium.org/

Great website design tips
http://www.unplug.com/great/

Net tips for writers and designers
http://www.dsiegel.com/tips/

A webmaster resource guide
http://www.web-authoring.com/

Webmonkey – general resources
http://hotwired.lycos.com/webmonkey/
webmonkey/

Access analysers

http://dir.yahoo.com/
Business_and_Economy/Companies/Comput-
ers/Business_to_Business/Software/Internet/
World_Wide_Web/Log_Analysis_Tools/Titles/

Hit List
http://www.accrue.com/products/

NetTracker
http://www.sane.com/

WebCounter Analysis
http://www.portset.co.uk/webcounter.htm

Authoring tools

http://dir.yahoo.com/
Computers_and_Internet/Software/Reviews/
Titles/Internet/Web_Authoring_Tools/
HTML_Editors/

Claris Home Page 3.0
http://www.clarishomepage.com

Macromedia Dreamweaver
http://www.macromedia.com/software/dreamweaver/

HoTMetaL Pro
http://www.sq.com

Microsoft Front Page
http://www.microsoft.com/frontpage/

Newsgroups

There are many newsgroups that you might want to take a look at, and once again, the following is just a selection. For an entire listing you should use your newsreader to display a list of them (you might need to check the newsreader's documentation for details on how to do this), or alternatively visit Deja.com at http://www.deja.com for more information on newsgroups.

alt.html

alt.html.critique

alt.html.editors.enhanced

alt.html.tags

alt.html.writers

alt.www.authoring

comp.infosystems.announce

comp.infosystems.www.authoring.html

comp.infosystems.www.authoring.tools

comp.infosystems.www.providers

comp.infosystems.www.users

comp.infosystems.www.misc

Glossary

Applets – A small program, often JavaScript, which does a very specific job such as display a date.

ASCII – American Standard Code for Information Interchange; straightforward text and numbers

Authoring tool – software that can be used to create Web pages and sites

Browser – software used to provide access to Web pages

CGI – Common Gateway Interface. Small program designed to take data from a web page and use it in one way or another

Domain name – name given to a website, usually in the format www.mysite.com (or co.uk etc.)

Frames – Web page that includes two or more separate windows which can be viewed and scrolled through independently of each other

FTP – File Transfer Protocol – utility for copying data from a local computer to a remote server

GIF – Graphics Interchange Format. One of two image formats recognised by browsers

Home Page – Web page designed to be the introduction to a web site

HTML – HyperText Mark up Language. The code or tags used to create a web page, which are instructions to a browser to tell it how to display the data contained on the page.

Hypertext – two separate pieces of information linked together so that it is possible to jump quickly from one to the other

Intranet – A internal network, usually running under Internet protocols, which is an organisation's 'internal internet'

Internet – A world wide network of computers which communicate with each other using the same (TCP/IP) protocol

JavaScript – Simple programming language to add flexibility and functionality to a web page

JPG (JPEG) – Joint Photographic Experts Group – an image format recognised by browsers

Microsoft Internet Explorer – see browser

Netscape – see browser

Search Engine – Internet resource used to find specific web pages

URL – Uniform Resource Locator – an address for a site or page, starting with http://

Web – The World Wide Web. Data published in pages linked together using HTML hyperlinks, accessible using the Internet

Web page – data set out in HTML format which can be viewed using a browser

Web site – collection of web pages at a specific URL

Aslib Know How Guides

Project Management for Library and Information Service Professionals

Researching for Business: Avoiding the 'Nice to Know' Trap

Strategic Planning for Library and Information Services

Teleworking for Library and Information Professionals

World Wide Web: How to Design and Construct Web Pages (2nd ed)

Printed and bound by CPI Group (UK) Ltd, Croydon, CR0 4YY

17/10/2024

01775689-0005